T0316718

Cambridge Elements ≡

Elements in Shakespeare Performance
edited by
W. B. Worthen
Barnard College

ROBERT LEPAGE'S INTERCULTURAL ENCOUNTERS

Christie Carson

Independent Scholar

CAMBRIDGE
UNIVERSITY PRESS

CAMBRIDGE
UNIVERSITY PRESS

University Printing House, Cambridge CB2 8BS, United Kingdom

One Liberty Plaza, 20th Floor, New York, NY 10006, USA

477 Williamstown Road, Port Melbourne, VIC 3207, Australia

314–321, 3rd Floor, Plot 3, Splendor Forum, Jasola District Centre,
New Delhi – 110025, India

79 Anson Road, #06–04/06, Singapore 079906

Cambridge University Press is part of the University of Cambridge.

It furthers the University's mission by disseminating knowledge in the pursuit of
education, learning, and research at the highest international levels of excellence.

www.cambridge.org
Information on this title: www.cambridge.org/9781108940481
DOI: 10.1017/9781108938730

First published 2021

A catalogue record for this publication is available from the British Library.

ISBN 978-1-108-94048-1 Paperback
ISSN 2516-0117 (online)
ISSN 2516-0109 (print)

Robert Lepage's Intercultural Encounters

Elements in Shakespeare Performance

DOI: 10.1017/9781108938730

First published online: February 2021

Christie Carson

Independent Scholar

Author for correspondence: Christie Carson, drchristiecarson@gmail.com

ABSTRACT: This study returns to the origins of Robert Lepage's directorial work and his first cross-cultural interaction with a Shakespearean text to provide some background for his later work. This early work is situated within the political and social context of Quebec and Canada in the 1980s. Constitutional wrangling and government policies of bilingualism, biculturalism and multiculturalism all had a profound impact on this director, helping to forge his priorities and working methods. In 2018 two of Lepage's productions were cancelled due to concerns about cultural appropriation. Lepage responded by stating his view that artists are above the concerns of political correctness. While this approach was deemed acceptable in the 1980s, this study looks at the dangers posed by approaching cross-cultural creation from this standpoint in the twenty-first century.

KEYWORDS: Shakespeare, Robert Lepage, Canadian theatre, Quebec theatre, Bilingual Shakespeare

ISBNs: 9781108940481 (PB), 9781108938730 (OC)

ISSNs: 2516-0117 (online), 2516-0109 (print)

Contents

1 The Boundaries of Shakespeare in Performance Criticism

This study has several aims. The first question it tackles is how to critically address the work of a director who has been engaged with Shakespeare's work, on occasion, across a long and illustrious career. Robert Lepage, the innovative and influential French-Canadian theatre director, is well known in theatre and performance circles, but when I mention his name to English-speaking Shakespeare colleagues, they often look at me quizzically. If his name is known, it is usually only in relation to either the production he directed of *A Midsummer Night's Dream* at the National Theatre in 1992 (in the mud) or his one-man show *Elsinore* from 1995 (Lepage's personal interaction with Shakespeare's *Hamlet*). But thinking in terms of inclusion and how the canon of performances that are taken seriously by the established Shakespearean critical world can be expanded to include productions from traditions that work outside of Anglo-American expectations, I want to take a closer look at the work of this director. Scholars who are interested in Shakespeare and Tourism (Bennett, 2005; Ormsby, 2017a, 2017b) have considered in some detail the works that are supported by international theatre festivals. But what about an artist like Lepage, who produces shows specifically for that international festival audience while working consistently from a base in Quebec City, drawing on traditions and expectations that are particularly Québécois?

The second aim of this work is to look at the issues of representation and responsibility which have recently become central to Shakespeare in performance studies and have circulated around Lepage's work for many years. The resurgence of an international discussion of racism in all areas of public and private life, particularly in response to the death of George Floyd in the United States, has brought to light accounts of earlier similar debates. In the same way, here I want to put forward an examination of older approaches to questions of inter/multi/trans/cross-cultural theatrical experiments as a means of exploring, if not explaining, how thoughts on these topics have developed over time. Can past productions and the critical dialogue that surrounded them be recuperated in a way that might make them useful to current debates? This argument comes in response to three recent volumes which have been published on Lepage's work: Melissa Poll's *Robert Lepage's Scenographic Dramaturgy: The Aesthetic Signature at Work*

(2018), James Reynolds's *Robert Lepage/Ex Machina: Revolutions in Theatrical Space* (2019), and Karen Fricker's *Robert Lepage's Original Stage Productions: Making Theatre Global* (2020). While the first of these studies examines Lepage's work on extant texts, it excludes his early career and includes only one serious examination of a Shakespeare performance. In the second volume, Reynolds tries to present an overview of Lepage's work and working practices from 1994 to 2018 but only glances at his work on Shakespeare. In the final volume, Fricker puts more emphasis on Lepage's origins (pre-1994) but restricts her examination to his original productions. Therefore, there is a large gap to be filled in terms of analysis of Lepage's controversial but influential Shakespeare productions in both English and French. Like these three authors, I engage with this director's process but I also want to examine the context from which this material springs. Rather than placing his work into larger international theoretical and artistic debates about theatrical space and visual forms of communication, I want to focus on how and where this director first approached Canada's bicultural debate through Shakespeare's text.

2 Liberal Humanism and the International Shakespeare Director

I do not contest the notion that Lepage's work speaks to European theatrical traditions and concerns, but here I argue that it also relies on dated claims of universalism and a sense of empathy for other cultures which is very much a product of Quebec's cultural history. One of the key issues to address when dealing with Lepage's Shakespeare productions is the fact that he is working in two different languages and with at least four different theatre traditions. While the critical writing that addresses his early work (coming largely out of English Canada) took this director to task for his somewhat cavalier approach to intercultural sensitivities (Carson, 1993, 2000; Fricker, 2003; Harvie, 2000; Hodgdon, 1996; Simon, 2000), the French-Canadian critical writing on this director and his company tended to elevate the position of the artist and the principle of artistic freedom in order to further nationalist ends. Entire volumes of Quebec theatre journals were dedicated to preserving this work, and the tone is more celebratory than critical. Later critical writing which responds to Lepage's internationally acclaimed productions coming out of Britain and France tends to see his work as a reaction to their own theatre traditions.[1] This is particularly true for Lepage's Shakespeare work, which has often been compared with Peter Brook's in terms of theatrical style. As the other celebrated bilingual (English/French) producer of Shakespeare dealing with intercultural issues and casts, the comparison seemed sensible, but I would argue it is reductionist for both directors. When considering the cultural contexts that nurtured these two directors, they could not be more different. Brook came from a background that was privileged both financially and educationally, attending private schools in England before studying at Oxford University. Lepage, by contrast, dropped out of high school without obtaining his diploma and went immediately to theatre school at the age of seventeen. Brook's parents were Russian and Jewish; Lepage's were French Canadian and Catholic. Brook was exposed to the theatre at an early age; Lepage was not. Brook began his career directing at the Royal Shakespeare Company before leaving the country to set up his own company in France. Lepage struggled to be heard as part of an embryonic Quebec theatre. Lepage's early Shakespeare work, and his work with intercultural collaboration and representation in Canada, provides a useful case study because of the way that it demonstrates his eclectic approach, which combines a mixture of existing performance styles. This director's work is notoriously difficult to sum up and even harder to restrict to one area of critical engagement[2], so here I focus my analysis on two early productions, *The Dragons' Trilogy* and *Romeo and Juliette* and their context, along with two recent ones, *SLĀV* and *Kanata*, which resulted in controversy, to highlight the issue of cultural representation and appropriation.

According to Fricker, avoiding critical definition has always been an aim of this theatre artist: 'This resistance to being classified is such a consistent

---

[1] See Fricker (2020) and Reynolds (2019) for a comprehensive account of Lepage criticism.

[2] Fricker (2020) makes it clear in her excellent summary of the critical perspectives that shed light on Lepage's work how difficult it is to categorise his productions critically.

position on Lepage's part that it has become definitional. This is a paradoxical stand – defining oneself by avoiding definition – and it is thus not surprising that paradox is a key term in discussions of Lepage's work' (2020: 2). This short piece will not try to pin him down, but rather it will highlight his originality while challenging his credentials as an intercultural director. There are not many internationally renowned directors of Shakespeare who also have directed Peter Gabriel's concerts and Cirque de Soleil's world tours. Directors at the Metropolitan Opera rarely also produce Shakespeare at the National Theatre in London. Lepage has had a unique position in the theatre world, and the way that his career has intersected with and employed the Shakespeare canon is unusual, even potentially unprecedented. But like Fricker, I want to examine exactly those issues that Lepage is keen to avoid: 'representational, authorial and corporate responsibility' (2020: 8). 'Paradox' is the word she uses in her analysis of Lepage, but she also points out that once 'pushed beyond its breaking point, a paradox becomes a contradiction' (2020: 8). This study highlights how different Lepage's work is from that of Brook, to illustrate how what was paradoxically similar has become a contradiction. The key point of overlap between these two directors, for the purposes of this argument, is their mutual attachment to older approaches to representation and responsibility.

Thus this study, like Fricker's, aims to raise the problem of critical categorisation, but in this case, I would like to argue for Lepage's inclusion in the canon of significant Shakespearean directors not because his work has been linked to Brook's but because of the way it differs from this other noted bilingual director. The mutual interest these two directors have in the concepts surrounding interculturalism and their approach to an image-oriented epic form of theatre-making have inspired comparisons between the two. But where their approaches diverge is in their approach to language and extant text. I would also suggest that Lepage's work on Shakespeare cannot be taken out of the context of this artist's extremely varied body of theatre productions. This analysis provides both a personal perspective and one that is grounded in a particular historical situation that aims to augment recent work by Poll (2018), Reynolds (2019) and Fricker (2020) by adding an analysis of his intercultural work and its reception that bookends the period these critics consider.

3 The Global Pandemic as a Spotlight

The combination of a world pandemic and international protests about systemic racism provide an extraordinary moment of clarity about current and possible future directions for the study of Shakespeare and performance in general and Lepage's work in particular. Theatre is under threat like never before. But the kind of theatre that Lepage and his companies (first Théâtre Repère and then Ex Machina) have created for the past three decades, which is designed for export to the international festival circuit, must face a foundational reconsideration. The pandemic lockdown created a perfect storm of circumstances which challenge the viability of the kind of social gathering that his theatre depends on. In the short-run, online distribution of past performances created a sense of plenty and prosperity for theatre audiences worldwide, as companies were able to gain wider recognition and access through free distribution of their work. According to Fricker, Lepage is a 'paradigmatic figure in the contemporary, globalised performance arts' because his productions deal directly with the huge changes that his audiences have experienced; they are 'productions that reflect spectators' privileged experiences of navigating contemporary globalisation' (2020: 6). But this work did not anticipate the pandemic, which has brought questions to light that have for too long hovered around the edges of criticism of international Shakespeare performance. What Fricker says about globalisation is even more true of the experience of life in lockdown for many:

> While bringing new experiences, wealth, and pleasures to some, however, the benefits of globalisation are not shared equally; globalisation has reified divisions of class, status, and power among the world's population. The increased movement of resources, ideas, and bodies under the conditions of globalisation is raising complex questions about responsibilities, affiliations, and ownership. (2020: 6)

For directors like Lepage, the pandemic signals a radical moment for rethinking a theatre which depends on international travel and elite audiences.

For Brook, who is in his nineties, there is no need for reinvention. His approach to performance is well documented critically, largely because of his own publications, through which he makes clear his aims and goals (something that Lepage has never done). His most recent volume, *Tip of the Tongue* (2017), written at the age of ninety-two, is particularly useful in highlighting the difference between these two men. Brook loves and trusts language; Lepage sees language as a curtain draped around culture that can be used to divide and confuse. The subtitle of Brook's book, *Reflections on Language and Meaning*, is the core of what separates the theatre of Lepage from the elder statesman of the theatre, particularly in terms of their Shakespeare direction. Brook is steeped in traditional literary approaches to Shakespeare and performance coming out of Oxford and the Royal Shakespeare Company, even when he rebels against them. Lepage has no training and very little interest in these traditions. His reputation as the next Peter Brook came from his production at the National Theatre in London of *A Midsummer Night's Dream* in English and *Le Cycle de Shakespeare: Macbeth, Coriolan, La Tempête* in French, which toured Europe from 1992 to 1994. But Lepage's initial interaction with bilingual Shakespeare was rather more problematic. His first foray into cross-cultural collaboration within Canada, while directing Shakespeare, took place on a much smaller scale in Saskatoon, Saskatchewan, in 1989, in a production of *Romeo and Juliet* which he co-directed with Gordon McCall. Working for the first time on a Shakespeare play outside Quebec and in English, a clash of cultures was perhaps inevitable. This early experiment did not foreshadow the extremely popular and critically acclaimed Shakespeare productions that were staged just three years later. An examination of the processes involved in Lepage's earliest work with Shakespeare can shed some light on his approach to language and cultural representation, revealing a deeply politically motivated approach, despite his denial of any interest in politics.

4 Developing Methods of Creation and Criticism

To understand where the inspiration for Lepage's internationally celebrated Shakespeare productions came from it is essential to look more closely at

Lepage's first global success, *The Dragons' Trilogy*. By analysing the working methods of this director in his home environment, taking into account the social and political context of this period in Canadian history, it is possible to see why Lepage found his Shakespearean voice in both languages and on national and international stages in the early 1990s. In 1992, working in both English and French, presenting his work on large established national and international stages, Lepage was stepping out of the alternative theatre in Quebec for the first time and into the international Shakespearean circuit of renowned directors that included not just Brook but others working on intercultural issues. Sherry Simon presents the accepted critical view that I am keen to challenge:

> The theatre of Robert Lepage is 'internationalized' in its very essence. Lepage has invented productions which, though constructed out of materials gathered from local contexts, are put together into performances that transcend these origins. This use of cultural collage places Lepage in the company of 'intercultural' theater artists Eugenio Barba, Peter Brook, Robert Wilson and Ariane Mnouchkine (Pavis 1). These directors have all used elements of distant cultures like the *Noh* tradition, *Kathakali* dancing from India, or African performances, as elements of their own theater. Like the other directors mentioned, Lepage uses the clash of traditions to construct his plays and *mise-en-scène*. (2000: 217)

Similarly, Andy Lavender makes a direct comparison between Lepage and two of these directors in his book *Hamlet in Pieces: Shakespeare Revisited by Peter Brook, Robert Lepage and Robert Wilson* (2001) using the response of each of these auteurs to Shakespeare's great play as a guiding principle. As a director himself, Lavender delves into the working process of each director and tries to adapt his critical approach in a way that is appropriate.

Both of these critics seek to elevate and explain Lepage's work through comparison to older more established directors. Alexandar Dundjerović, himself a director and an immigrant to Canada, looks at the way that Brook and Lepage are connected through their approach to older theatrical forms;

'Like the theatre of Peter Brook, Lepage's theatre blurs the traditional boundaries between rehearsal and performance, transforming them into one continuous creative process' (2007: x). But Dundjerović also looks to locate Lepage in his own social context and tries to define his work through its rehearsal and performance practices. Fricker points out why context is key when analysing this work:

> Alongside this broader framing of Lepage's work within shifting conceptions of contemporary theatre directing, it is also useful to place his practice specifically in the context of Québécois culture and theatrical practices. Understanding the relationship between Lepage and his particular milieu sheds light on the fundamentals of his approach, and also usefully complicates a tendency to describe him as exceptional when in fact his is part of an evolving tradition. (2020: 29)

This analysis combines these approaches to look at Lepage's early work and context but compares this director to himself. By creating a comparison between his work directing Shakespeare, in a cross-cultural production, with his work devising a new production with Théâtre Repère at around the same time, it is possible to develop a critical method which may suit other directors who approach both Shakespeare and their own devised work. The assumption in Shakespeare performance criticism is often to question what directors have brought to 'our' understanding of the texts but here I want to look at what Shakespeare's dramaturgy has done for this director. By choosing to tackle Shakespeare, in more than one language and one country, Lepage positioned himself quite differently in the Anglo-American critical world and in the European theatrical critical tradition. The role of the artist in the European tradition is based on the notion that the director is more than simply an interpreter of the texts. The tradition of the auteur in the French press and critical discourse is central to understanding responses to Lepage's work outside Canada. Looking at his work in this way helps explain why the comparison with Brook has been so enduring but also why it needs to end.

5 Challenges for the Twenty-First-Century Artist and Critic

In the twenty-first century, the role of both the artist and the critic is changing, and another aim of this analysis is to trace how these changes are taking place using Lepage as a case study. While times have changed, in many ways, Lepage's working method has not altered as much as it could or should have. Because his career was linked to the reputation of older directors' work, Lepage benefitted from the expectations audiences had for the work of an earlier generation. But his insistence on the special place of the artist in society (and the special place of Quebec within in Canadian society) reached an impasse in 2018. Two productions, one depicting African American slaves, $SL\bar{A}V$, and the other telling the stories of Canada's Indigenous people, *Kanata*, were criticised by members of these two artistic communities. Lepage's explanations for both performances centred around ideas of empathy and universal human truths. These legitimating strategies were seen as insulting, involving the erasure of the cultural communities whose stories were being told. *Kanata*, as a co-production with Adriane Mnouchkine's Théâtre du Soleil from Paris, was meant to show the coming together of two great intercultural directors. Instead, it highlighted the limitations of their ways of working and their attitudes towards the representation of others. In fact, while *Kanata* was cancelled entirely in Canada, an alternative version of this show was eventually staged in Paris, which focused on the importance of artistic freedom, demonstrating the difference between these two cultural communities.

However, this international performance did not allow Lepage to escape the controversy at home. Philip S. S. Howard, in a recent article about the controversy that surrounded Lepage's production of $SL\bar{A}V$, details the history of what he calls 'antiblackness' in Quebec, using this incident as an example. In essence, he critiques the performance of resistance inspired by this production and points to the underlying cultural and social trends that it highlights. The history Howard charts, of misguided efforts to include Black francophones in the nationalist project by the White community in Quebec, speaks of repeated attempts to erase difference out of a sense of universalist empathy. The notion that the White Québécois considered themselves *les Nègres blancs d'Amérique* (the White negroes/ni**ers/Blacks of America – Howard debates the translation) can certainly be seen as taking empathy too far and in entirely the wrong direction. But using the analysis of the reaction to a show the critic has not seen raises another problem that Lepage highlighted himself during the controversy: how can a critic participate in a debate when he has not heard what is being said on-stage? Given that Lepage's work is created in response to audience inter-action over time, how can it proceed when the audience refuses to engage in debate?

Like Howard, I want to look to the controversy around the cancellation of *SLĀV* and *Kanata*[3] as a means of pointing out that Lepage's work has come up against the limits of the liberal humanist notion of universality and intercultural theatre as it was critically defined at the end of the twentieth century. Like Howard, I did not see either of the performances in question and rely on accounts of the controversy that I have read from a distance, but this stands in contrast to my involvement with the two earlier case studies documented here. These are productions which I saw and researched in some detail, interviewing the participants and engaging with the interviews of others. The shift from active researcher, audience member and involved participant in the social and cultural struggles being depicted on stage to a faraway critic relying on mediated material to gain an understanding of an event I did not witness is also designed to make a point. It seems to me that this is the way that criticism of Shakespeare in performance is inevitably going. Having recently written a review for *Shakespeare Bulletin* of Lepage's *Coriolanus* at the Stratford Festival, which I saw live in 2018 and on my laptop in 2020, I am keenly aware of how recorded performances are inevitably stripped of context to some degree. If inclusion is about making experiences available, then my contribution to this debate must be to document what I was lucky enough to see and hear. Easy cross-comparisons between intercultural productions recorded and distributed online are challenged here by direct experience of the creative process and

---

[3] It is important to point out that *SLĀV* was performed several times before it was cancelled, and *Kanata* was staged in France to mixed critical and audience reception.

audience response in two specific cases and contexts which span a period of critical engagement in this work over a thirty-year period.

But am I swimming against the tide? Looking to the future, I wonder if the 'force' and 'authority of performance' that Worthen (1997, 2003) describes are dwindling, along with the possibility of creating an engaged embedded critical perspective. In the spirit of adding to knowledge and contributing my own experience to that which has been documented critically elsewhere, I rely on my account of being present at rehearsals and performances for the shows I document. Shakespeare in performance scholarship has expanded hugely over the past decade due to access to online resources, but I hope that attending live performances and interacting with practitioners in the real world will not become things of the past as a result. This account of the work of Lepage, then, aims to add to the existing critical examinations of this director in a way that is meant to fill in gaps and raise questions. I wish to challenge existing assumptions about the ways that Lepage is like Brook in order to define his work on its own terms. In addition to putting a marker in the sand for the early work of this director, this piece also aims to claim a bit of the Shakespearean landscape for directors, like Lepage, who do not necessarily fit the title of 'great Shakespeareans' but who have contributed to the breadth and depth of the work seen on the international stage. The critical approach taken will hopefully provide a model for other scholars who want to move theatre practitioners from their own cultural backgrounds from the edges into the accepted circle of influential practitioners, not on the coattails of other more celebrated theatre artists, but in their own right. If Shakespeare studies is to survive in the twenty-first century, then it must accept more diverse membership both in terms of the scholars who are writing and in terms of the topics tackled. The field must also be willing to look at difficult questions such as racism and cultural insensitivity, not just in the plays themselves but in the social and critical practices that have surrounded their staging over time.

6 The 2018 Controversies

Lepage, in his 2020 National Theatre Platform interview given just a few days before the pandemic lockdown, made a revealing statement:

'Theatre is the game of memory' (Lepage, 2020a). This comment made me realise that to me criticism is the game of remembering differently. The question which we have both had to address recently is our own cultural position and its legacy. In June 2018 Lepage's production of *Coriolanus* opened at the Stratford Festival to rave reviews. Finally, after forty years as a director, his work was seen on the most prestigious Canadian stage for Shakespeare performance. Within a month of this premiere, two of his largest projects were cancelled due to public outcry. The first, *SLĀV*, was part of the Montreal Jazz Festival and involved a collaboration with the singer Béatrice Bonifassi. It also involved several White actor/singers dressed as slaves, singing African American spiritual songs. The production was cancelled after three performances due to protests on the street and the withdrawal from the Festival of Moses Sumney, who called the production 'hegemonic, appropriative and neo-imperialistic' (2018). Given that Lepage has throughout his career consistently worked on projects that highlight cultural plurality, it was a surprise to him that after many years of internationally acclaimed professional work, he was accused of cultural appropriation and racism. American singer Sumney went on to make a statement that directly addresses the question, 'Why now?'

> The point you are missing is that there is no context in which white people performing black slave songs is okay. Especially not while they are dressed like poor field workers or cotton pickers. Especially not while they are directed by a white director and in a theatre charging loads of money. . . . This kind of black imitation is very reminiscent of blackface minstrel shows. The only thing missing is black paint. (Sumney, 2018)

Sumney makes clear that Lepage's view, and perhaps my own, which assumes access to the theatre to engage in the debate being put forward, is a false starting point.

   The *National Post* article that describes the controversy that took place in Montreal is illuminating in terms of the way the protest (performance?) was documented. Sumney announced on Twitter his decision to withdraw his show from the Festival and to perform instead at an alternative venue in Montreal. The Festival organisers and Lepage and Bonifassi took the unusual step of publishing their response statements on Facebook, links to which are included in a *National Post* article (Lepage & Bonifassi, 2018). The video, which is placed at the top of the article page online (from YouTube), shows the demonstrators outside the theatre blocking the entrance for patrons, flanked by the police. Like Howard's piece, the *National Post* article focuses primarily on the views of people who did not see the show. To Lepage, this was artistic censorship. In his joint statement with Bonifassi, he suggests that their motivation was to heal rather than to antagonise: 'Diversity and its artistic potential are at the heart of *SLĀV* as much as the legacy of slavery. Do we have the right to tell these stories? Audience members will have the opportunity to decide after having seen the show' (Lepage & Bonifassi, 2018). Looking at Lepage's question 'Who has the right of representation?' is a key aim of this piece. Another is to tackle the wider question: how has the relationship between the artist, the critic and the audience changed in the twenty-first century as a result of the circulation of information on social media as well as through the mainstream press? Throughout this controversy, Lepage's production of *Coriolanus* continued to be performed on the Avon stage in Stratford, Ontario, to full houses. This paradox is one which I feel can be answered by looking at the fact that English Canadian critics had always critiqued Lepage's approach to representation and his production of this particular play provided a form of an answer to the critics he faced in Quebec at the time. In this *Coriolanus*, the 'people' were not given a voice on stage. In his *Shakespeare Bulletin* review of the production, Manuel Antonio Jaquez points this out: 'mass media replaced the tangible citizenry of Rome as the key opponent and critic of Coriolanus's views and demeanor' (2019: 113). Lepage, like Coriolanus, was displaying his disdain for 'the people' on stage in Stratford while audiences protested in Montreal.

A different sort of protest came about in response to Lepage's next project, *Kanata*, a sweeping epic about the history of Canada and the relationship between the Indigenous people and the settlers. This time it was a collective of Indigenous artists who came together to write an open letter in *Le Devoir* newspaper, asking why their stories were being told by others. It was a call for collaboration and involvement rather than a request to cancel the production, but this was the final outcome. The open letter of the artists was addressed to the French theatre director, Mnouchkine, and it was specifically in response to an interview that she had given in the same paper. The statement reads:

> Madame Mnouchkine a exploré nos territoires, elle n'a plus besoin de nos services. Exit ! Elle aime nos histoires, mais n'aime pas nos voix. Il nous semble que c'est une répétition de l'histoire et de tels agissements nous laissent un certain sentiment de déjà-vu. On nous inventera, on nous mimera, on nous racontera, parce qu'elle a compris, parce qu'ils ont compris. Pardonnez notre cynisme, mais avons-nous vraiment été compris ?

> *Ms Mnouchkine has explored our lands, but she has no more use of our services. Exit! She likes our stories, but not our voices. It seems to us that history is repeating itself, and such wrongdoing gives us a certain sense of déjà-vu. They will invent us, mime us, tell our stories, because she understands us, because they understand us. Forgive our cynicism, but have we really been understood?*[4] (Aubin-Dubois et al., 2018)

After a six-hour meeting with representatives of the group trying to find common ground, Mnouchkine and Lepage announced that the production would not go forward. And still *Coriolanus* in Stratford continued, reinforcing the notion that Lepage's work on Shakespeare stands apart from his collective created intercultural work but also that an elite Festival audience was prepared to put up with and even support his universalist views if the show they were watching did not upset *them*.

Lepage's statement on Facebook in response to the furore tries to address the issue of artistic freedom in a way that highlights his liberal humanist position:

---

[4] All quotations originally published in French have been translated by Lynne Rickards.

> Since the dawn of time, theatre has been based on a very simple principle, that of playing someone else. Pretending to be someone else. Stepping into the shoes of another person to try to understand them, and in the process, perhaps understanding ourselves, better. This ancient ritual requires that we borrow, for the duration of the performance, someone else's look, voice, accent and at times even gender.
>
> But when we are no longer allowed to step into someone else's shoes, when it is forbidden to identify with someone else, theatre is denied its very nature, it is prevented from performing its primary function and is thus rendered meaningless. (Lepage, 2018)

Howard highlights the fact that in French this statement uses the phrase 'slipping into another's skin' in place of 'stepping into the shoes of another' and points out the implications of this shift: 'By speaking of slipping into the other's skin in the context of the $SL\bar{A}V$ debate, Lepage admits an attempt to inhabit Blackness as a vehicle through which to understand himself and others who are not Black' (2020: 135).

It is this point, the function and meaning of intercultural theatre, that needs to be addressed. I believe that an examination of two of Lepage's early projects, one that is Shakespearean and one that is not, illustrates the way his collaborative work is constructed and the origins of the problem that erupted in 2018. The approach taken focuses on the freedom of the artist to represent the Other, with the accompanying freedom, even the objective to offend or to provoke. Comparing this early work to the projects of recent years, I suggest that little has changed in Lepage's outlook or approach, steeped as they are in a debate about bilingualism, biculturalism and multiculturalism, as they were defined in Canada in the late 1980s. What has changed is his position, reputation, international influence, and resultant responsibility. In addition, the explosion of social media in the twenty-first century, which allows everyone (who can afford the technology) access to self-expression, has resulted in greater scrutiny of his production choices and less tolerance of his universalising stance.

While in his 2018 statement Lepage rages against the ill-informed response to his work, I argue that earlier work could be seen to suffer from similar issues, although he was not always held to account for them at the time. The aim here is not merely to find fault with Lepage's approach, but rather to situate it in temporally and culturally specific terms. The beginning of his intercultural journey defined this end-point long before it was reached. As Howard makes clear, Quebec identity and sense of nationhood have always been linked to the arts and, in particular, to the theatre as a means of nation building: 'Of course, nation building is an inherently racial project, and therefore it follows that the arts in Quebec also serve to narrate and construct its particular racialized social relations with 'cultural communities,' even if this is done in the name of openness and egalitarianism – that is, interculturalism' (2020: 128).

Ultimately Howard is making the same point in 2020 that I made in my 1993 PhD dissertation at the University of Glasgow (*"True" Interculturalism: Experiments in Intercultural Theatre in Canada and Scotland*), although I was interested in Lepage's view of language as a marker of culture rather than his view of those who are racially other. Howard states: 'Quebec makes its nationalist claims through universalization, and the erasure of difference' (2020: 128); 'the Quebec state has repeatedly forged its linguistic and nationalist identity against Blackness under the guise of commonality while demeaning and/or erasing Blackness' (2020: 132). While Howard speaks to the racial elements of the province's and Lepage's vision of national identity, I highlight the linguistic aspects of the debate. Quebec identity is formed in opposition to that which has been identified as Anglophone culture, and so the position of Shakespeare's work in that debate is interesting critically since English in this view stands for British, American and English Canadian culture simultaneously, a generalisation I challenge.

7 The Artist in Canada: Representing Difference

Quebec has always had its own approach to the development of culture, which differentiated it from the rest of Canada, and only part of this difference stems from the issue of language. The devolution of provincial powers in the area of culture means that Quebec has always had different priorities and funding models. Some of these differences were motivated by pragmatic issues, such as the geographic spread of English speaking theatre artists, who travel and work across the entirety of the second-largest country in the world, compared with the relatively compact geography of Quebec. Other issues came out of the fact that the two language communities have not only different mother tongues (English and French) but motherlands (Britain and France) and therefore different cultural histories as well. The focus on Shakespeare in English Canada, particularly in Ontario and at the Stratford Festival, since it was first established in 1953, was contrasted by an early focus on Molière, Racine, Feydeau and other French masters in Quebec (as seen through parody in Lepage's 1998 film *Nô*). However, because Shakespeare's work is lyrical and image oriented, as well as engaged with issues of political power, it became the subject of interest in Quebec from the time of the Quiet Revolution, the separatist movement of the 1960s and 1970s.[5] The fact that Shakespeare was performed in translation and was not seen as a core part of the cultural heritage of Quebec gave theatre artists more freedom to radically alter these plays in performance.

Nationalism in English Canada in the 1960s was focused on creating a new flag and an identity for the country as a whole that distinguished it from Britain and the United States. In this way, Shakespeare formed part of the Loyalist narrative which claimed English literary heritage as a defining feature. This movement towards a unified nationalist ideal based on the English language and culture made the population in Quebec feel alienated and discussions of separation soon began. By the 1970s, these discussions had become violent action, which saw the kidnapping of prominent citizens and bombs being set off in public places. During this period, Quebec looked to France and the rest of the world to support its bid for freedom and independence, so investing money and energy in promoting its own artists outside of the country was a politically motivated act. By contrast, in

---

[5] Fricker points to the 'political, economic, social, and cultural autonomy experienced' at the time and calls the Quiet Revolution a 'period of rapid change, modernization, and national self-realisation' (2020: 29).

English Canada there was a greater focus on trying to acquaint artists across the country with each other, to further the politically motivated goal of defining a common history and culture across an expansive geography.

In the early 1980s, a great deal of energy politically was spent by Prime Minister Pierre Trudeau (father of Justin Trudeau) to establish a Canadian constitution. This seemingly straightforward task, to bring the highest authority in the land to the people of the country, was the subject of a bitter battle between Quebec and the other Provinces. Several attempts were made to include Quebec in the new constitution, but all of them failed. The result of this is a constitution that excludes one of the two largest Provinces in the country, Quebec became a 'stateless nation' (Fricker, 2020: 1). Not surprisingly, this led to an increased sense that the country contained two nations with two separate national identities – the *Two Solitudes*, as defined by Hugh MacLennan in his 1945 novel. While there continue to be calls for independence and a separatist party in Quebec (the Bloc Québécois which gains seats in the national Parliament), a referendum to leave the union has never obtained enough votes to break the country apart. But this rupture continues to be a very real threat.

So as the 1980s turned into the 1990s in Quebec, the political battlefield which threatened to break the country apart changed two aspects of national identity formation in the country: first, the vision of the nation from within, and second, the relationship between Canada and the rest of the world. Given that all attempts to find a unified culture had failed, a shift occurred which saw the diversity of the nation as a strength to be embraced rather than a flaw to be condemned. The former defensiveness and insularity in English Canada, which sought uniformity, were replaced by an acceptance of difference and tolerance. With a more relaxed sense of self, Canada was ready to meet the world. The international community ceased to be a hostile and conflictual arena and was seen instead as a place of open discussion and communication. Given that many immigrant communities had fled war-torn environments for the safe harbour of Canada, the focus initially of national identity formation was on defining and defending the country's borders culturally from both European and American influences. The national motto of 'Peace, Order and Good Government' was not as exciting as the American equivalent, but it illustrated the country's aspirations;

security, stability and prosperity for all. So by the end of the twentieth century, artists performing abroad were supported from all regions of the country, allowing the international theatre audience to appreciate the breadth of approaches coming out of the nation during a time of developing self-awareness and cultural confidence for Canadian artists abroad.

Robert Lepage has consistently claimed that his work is not political but his vision of the world was formed during the early struggle for self-definition in Quebec. The recognition he sought was first within the province, then through national and international touring. While Poll's and Reynolds's critical interest in the work of this director focuses on his work from the mid-1990s, when his international reputation began, here I want to focus instead on the early germination of his work and on two productions which consider the clash of cultures, both figurative and real, of the different cultural communities within Canada. The first, *The Dragons'* *Trilogy* (1985), considered the experience of the Chinese Canadian community across three generations, and the second, a bilingual production of Shakespeare's *Romeo and Juliet* (1989) co-directed with Gordon McCall of Shakespeare on the Saskatchewan Theatre, brought together a French-speaking company of actors to play the Capulets and an English-speaking company to play the Montagues. These two productions illustrate Lepage's developing methods of creation and early ideas about cultural collaboration within the Canadian context in the 1980s and 1990s.

In the latter half of the 1980s and the beginning of the 1990s, theatres across Canada were tackling changing demographics in their audiences. The theatre communities of English- and French-Canada reacted by trying to create productions which spoke to intercultural questions from a position that was less directed towards unifying nationalist aims and more towards exploring differences of opinion and outlook. What came out of this period was what might be called 'multicultural' theatre. As in politics, multiculturalism in the theatre presents cross-cultural projects where there was a seeming openness, in that spokespeople of minority groups are involved in creating images of themselves on stage. However, often the real power and the purse strings were still in the hands of the group which instigated these projects. The result was often well-intentioned but unbalanced collaborative efforts which stayed on the surface of the issues addressed by 'true' interculturalism, which Richard Schechner defined during the same period as encounters 'where different cultures and peoples each take a fair share of economic and political power' (Schechner, 1992: 7). While the debate about what constitutes intercultural theatre has moved on considerably (see Gilbert and Tompkins, 1996, and especially Knowles, 2010), Lepage's early work can be seen to be very much part of this well-intentioned approach to difference, although he tried to differentiate this work through the use of visual imagery and multiple languages. Lepage's description of 'slipping into the skin of another' which Howard highlights is evident here in literal terms in the performance of Chinese characters by French Canadian actors in the *Trilogy* without explanation or apology.

In contrast to the well-meaning but misplaced sympathies of multi-culturalism's involvement of token 'others', Lepage's theatre seemed initially to achieve a complex reaction to the question of how to deal with language in an intuitive way. Lepage set out a vision of a plural world, given his theatre often avoided language altogether by relying instead on images to convey meaning. This approach came as a challenge to the theatre artists of English Canada, who had relied almost entirely on the written text to create a representative theatre tradition, using Shakespeare as their literary inspiration. What Lepage's work helped instigate was a reassessment of the idea of a canon of written work as an illustration of the continuance and success of the theatre community, enabling a shift to a vision of the canon as an ongoing, ephemeral body of work that takes place in the theatres throughout the country. Lepage's multilingual image-based work was seen as an ideal example of theatre which could speak to all of the communities of Canada, even if it spoke differently to those groups. Lepage's approach to language came from his own bilingual upbringing. The split vision of the country was not just a political position for Lepage but a reality of his everyday life.[6] As Lepage himself pointed out recently, bilingualism and biculturalism were not just government policies but were part of the fabric of his upbringing (Lepage, 2020a). Dundjerović says, 'Lepage liked to see his family, with its bilingual mix, as "a metaphor for Canada,

[6] Robert and his sister Lynda spoke French at home with their biological parents, but his two older adopted siblings spoke English.

a cultural metaphor'" (2007: 5). While this metaphoric approach sounds inclusive, it is important to note that his household was bi-cultural, not multi-cultural, and so imposing his own experience onto the entire country was inevitably going to cause problems.

In looking at two case studies of work which involved Lepage and Théâtre Repère during the 1980s, a time of enormous political upheaval, I want to illustrate this director's initial approach to the question of a cross-cultural debate. The position of Shakespeare's work in the debate about English and French-Canadian theatre culture is fundamental, given that both groups approached this playwright's work from very different perspectives. *The Dragons' Trilogy*, developed entirely by Théâtre Repère with a White French Canadian cast in Quebec City, was an imagistic, non-text-based piece which relied, in a universalist sense, on the transferability of visual images. The English-Canadian project was a bilingual production of Shakespeare's *Romeo and Juliette*[7] that took an established text and imbued it with cross-cultural and bilingual sensibilities related to the specific English/ French and West/East divide in Canada. These projects demonstrate how a similar desire to produce theatre that crossed cultural borders created two very different productions, but productions which were representative of the outlooks of the communities which engendered them. These shows prove illuminating in terms of Lepage's later work on Shakespeare in both languages and on the international stage.

To give a sense of the social reality of the English- and French-speaking theatre communities, I begin with an examination of the creative process involved in the two projects. I then provide a critical assessment of 'multi-culturalism' as a government policy, and finally, I question the biases and hierarchies at play in the projects under examination. In Quebec during this period, *interculturalism* was the more widely accepted term and *collective collaboration* was the most frequently employed approach when creating theatre that tackled cultural differences. Looking at the development of Lepage's later work, these priorities were reinforced and even entrenched. The purpose of returning to these two early case studies is to reveal the

---

[7] The change in the play's title was designed to reflect the bilingual casting of the show.

faults, problems and imbalances which were inherent in this work and to demonstrate the cultural prejudices which held these linguistic communities back from creating productions that allowed for an equitable sharing of creative input and power. As early experiments in intercultural communication, these two quite different projects provide a back story, or point of origin, for Lepage's later work on Shakespeare which gained international exposure and attention. Ultimately I assert that Lepage suffered and continues to suffer from what Fricker describes as the 'fetishising [of] an abstract claim of otherness as somehow definitional of being Quebecois' (2020: 21) which has allowed him to ignore degrees of otherness within the Province that require representation.

8 The Cultural and Theatrical Climate in Canada, 1980–1992

As the 1970s turned into the 1980s, the buoyancy and cultural optimism of the earlier decade quickly dissipated. Following the narrow 'Non' vote in Quebec on sovereignty association in 1980, nationalist sentiments went into decline. A recession in both parts of the country and a Conservative government coming to power in the 1980s also went a long way to dampen the spirits, and reduce the budgets, of theatre companies. How each of these communities reacted to these events determined the progress of their theatre communities over the next decade. In looking at the theatrical activity in Quebec and English Canada between 1980 and 1992, it is possible to show how each of these communities dealt with the challenges of increasing cultural diversity and decreasing state funding.

Ironically, the failure of the separatist movement to gain enough support for sovereignty did not lead to elation and relaxation on the subject of the country's united future. In fact, it had the opposite effect. Because the votes to stay in Canada became increasingly close (in 1980, 59.56 per cent to 40.44 per cent, and in 1995, 50.58 per cent to 49.42 per cent), these referenda highlighted just how precarious the union of the nation called Canada was. The 1980 referendum began a process of reassessment and analysis of what the country was to become that was to rage for the next two decades. In 1982, Prime Minister Pierre Trudeau and the provincial Premiers created Canada's constitution. (Until that time, Canada had been ruled by the

British North America Act, an Act of the British Parliament.) What Trudeau (senior) managed to do was to create a Canadian constitution, with an entrenched Charter of Rights and Freedoms, that had the agreement of all of the Provinces, except Quebec. This exclusion was seen by Quebec as further proof that Canada was a unity of which it had no part. While the politicians scurried around trying to rectify this problem, after the failure of two later constitutional accords (Meech Lake in 1990 and the Charlottetown Agreement in 1992), Canada still possesses a constitution which has not been ratified by Quebec (the 'stateless nation'). Ironically, Pierre Trudeau, whose pride and joy was this constitution and who was himself French-Canadian and entirely bilingual, was seen by many at the start of his time in power as the man who would bring about the changes Quebec wanted in the federal political system. This was not to be, and Trudeau antagonised many voters in the process, particularly in the Western provinces, by seeming to be too centrist in his approach and too partial in dealing with the demands of Quebec.

The failure of the Charlottetown Accord (six of the ten provinces and one territory voted in the 1992 Referendum to reject the Accord) was a setback both for strong federalists and for the separatist movement in Quebec. Even though no agreement of any kind was reached (or perhaps because of this fact), the period of the 1980s and the early 1990s stimulated a decade of discussion, negotiation and controversy over the future of the country. It also clarified in the minds of both English-speaking and French-speaking Canadians the position of each side, clearly demonstrating the incompatibility of these two ways of seeing the country. Quebec has always seen itself as one of two founding nations; English Canada, by contrast, saw the country as a confederation of ten provinces. The rest of Canada was seen by Quebec as a monolith (*R.O.C.* as it was affectionately called), but what the constitutional negotiations pointed out quite clearly was that the rest of Canada was far from unified and could not agree among its nine parties on any of the key issues at stake. The Western provinces, in particular, with their own resources (oil primarily) wanted more autonomy than Trudeau was willing to give them. The divisions and diversity in the country grew rather than diminished with greater debate. English Canada became an umbrella term which encompassed a wide range of older and newer immigrant populations. The relationship between the English language and a unifying culture was strained. Tolerance of difference became the only defining national trait that could gain acceptance by all, even though it was differently interpreted across the nation. Shakespeare's work was not representative culturally for a large percentage of the population, yet these plays continued to play a pivotal role.

The effects of the political instability of the 1980s in the theatre in Canada were significant but differently articulated in English and French Canada. Robert Wallace describes the state of theatrical cross-fertilisation between Montreal and Toronto as an indication of differing aesthetic points of view, which reflect the differing political outlooks (1990: 38). He notes that the traffic between these two cities was mostly one way, from Montreal to Toronto. This, he says, was for two reasons. The first came out of the trend established early in the 1970s of confidence in Quebec in its cultural product and the desire to show this culture off outside the province. This strategy in marketing worked internationally as well as in the rest of Canada. Theatres in Ontario took little interest in Québécois theatre in the 1970s (the work of Michel Tremblay being one notable exception), but in the 1980s, suddenly English-Canadian audiences began to see a great deal of French-Canadian work. This was, in part, due to the increase in festival activity in Toronto, but there were more complex reasons which Wallace explains resulted from differing visions of culture across Canada. In Montreal, there was a general lack of interest in what was going on in English Canada. This can be illustrated by the fact that the number of plays translated from French to English far exceeded the number of plays translated from English to French at this time. This was widely accepted as an indication that English Canadian work was inferior to the work being generated in Quebec, but Wallace gives another explanation:

> Quebec theatres look not just to Canada for plays to translate and produce, but to the entire English-speaking world –
> indeed, to plays written in other languages besides English.
> The priorities of many of these theatres are shaped by trends
> in international performance, not by the principle of Canadian
> content. (1990: 38)

Because Quebec had, in this moment, no particular loyalty to Canada nor to the English language, there was no incentive to look to English Canada for work to produce. In Quebec, the search was for theatrical innovation and drama which expressed an international social reality, and in these terms, an insular English Canadian theatre had little to offer.

This attitude was in sharp contrast to the view shared by theatres in Toronto and the rest of English Canada, a fact which Wallace makes clear: 'In [English] Canada, it is important to produce Canadian playwrights first. And for most of them, plays from Quebec, once they are translated into English, are Canadian. Indeed, most of Toronto's not-for-profit theatres are more interested in moving Canadian plays across the country than in touring artists around the world' (1990: 38). This trend shows the development of a spirit which began in the 1970s, an interest in creating and maintaining a specifically (English) Canadian culture for audiences in Canada by placing emphasis and importance on local or regional events. This tendency, according to Wallace, made English-Canadian theatre more 'Canadian' in the sense that it sought to reflect local reality rather than global concerns. Conversely, the prevailing attitude in Quebec theatre made it more international. He describes the differing attitudes of theatre directors and producers in the two parts of the country:

> By and large, Montreal theatres produce plays by Québécois writers whereas Toronto theatres present plays by Canadians across the country. Concomitantly, Toronto theatre is much more insular than that of Montreal. Festivals of international work, for example, are few and are much less popular than the Quebec festivals that attract huge crowds. (1990: 39)

Thus the cultural and political attitudes in the country at the time which kept these two traditions apart had a great effect on the theatre. Ideally, as Wallace points out, a bilingual theatre would have evolved where artists and audiences would feel comfortable with either language, but this for the most part did not occur. Language represented two opposing political positions which the theatre helped to keep apart.

9 Bilingual Theatre in Canada

In order to situate the production of *Romeo and Juliette* examined here, it is important to say a little bit about bilingual theatre in Canada, as well as the relationship between bilingual theatre and the production of Shakespeare's plays. Bilingual theatre, which includes the country's two official languages, might seem the most natural and most Canadian form possible, but the intensity of the antagonism between these two groups has been such that the 'two solitudes' have developed in isolation. The federal policy of bilingualism and biculturalism (which became law with the *Official Languages Act* of 1969), while recognising the existence of two cultures, did little to integrate these two warring groups of people. That is not to say that attempts to express and convey the emotions and experiences involved in a country with two founding languages have not been made. There have been some efforts in that direction, but they have been few and far between and have always provoked considerable controversy.

The most famous attempt to address the issue of bilingualism through a Shakespearean production took place in 1956, under a tent, by the Avon River in Stratford, Ontario. But when English-Canadian actors standing in for the British army faced French-Canadian actors, representing the French nobility, in Shakespeare's *Henry V*, the French actors spoke the lines as written, so were heard to articulate their position predominantly in accented English. Martin Hunter describes this production:

> The first truly Canadian production on the Stratford Festival
> stage was the 1956 *Henry V*. The ailing, wild-eyed king of
> France, Gratien Gélinas, was backed up by the acerbic power
> of Jean Gascon's Constable; the rest of the French court was
> a band of capering, mercurial young actors from Montreal's
> Théâtre du Nouveau Monde. Together they provided a perfect
> foil for the arrogant underplaying of Christopher Plummer,
> the Westmount boy who believed in his divine right to rule.
> (1987: 18)

The mention of Westmount, the expensive Anglophone area of Montreal, and the name of Christopher Plummer present a clear sense of what English

Canada stood for at this time for a French-Canadian audience: wealth, privilege and entitlement. Less well known might be the importance of the King of France being played by Gratien Gélinas, a noted Quebec political playwright, and the appearance of Jean Gascon, an important Québécois theatre director.

Hunter goes on to relate the passionate response of the on-stage action and its reception by a mixed audience in Ontario in the 1950s:

> Gascon recently recalled that the French actors had to learn their parts phonetically, but no one had to teach them the feelings of fury and frustration that made their performances take fire. Here, on stage at last, was a confrontation as elemental as the one I'd observed ten years earlier in a game between the [Toronto] Maple Leafs and the [Montreal] Canadiens, when the passion of the players in their symbolic uniforms – true blue for the Leafs, blood crimson for the Canadiens – outdid anything I'd ever felt in any theatre. (1987: 18)

Hunter's enthusiasm makes it clear that for many this was seen as a landmark production, a starting point for a new kind of Canadian theatre that could join the two linguistic groups:

> *Henry V* was hailed as a sort of flagship production for Canadian theatre, a model that would bring to our stages the excitement and conflict already bubbling just below the placid surface of Canadian life. Subsequent history did not see this prophecy fulfilled. Plummer went on to stardom in London and New York, and Gascon became the first Canadian artistic director of Stratford. (1987: 18)

But this production was not the only effort made to unite the two theatre worlds. The National Theatre School was set up in Montreal with the hope that young actors training together would go on to work together. While there were separate programmes for English- and French-speaking actors, they shared voice, movement and mask classes. This was arranged in the hope that it would build bridges. Theatre critic Herbert Whittaker recalls, 'We hoped it might lead to a new Canadian style that would marry the vivacity of the French with the intellectual rigor of the English' (quoted in Hunter, 1987: 18). But these hopes were not fulfilled, and to this day the two programmes are linguistically divided.

The bilingual theatre that has, on occasion, arisen has been used not to express a coming together of the two language groups, but rather as an explanation of the hostilities which kept the two groups apart. The first text which was written to describe a bilingual environment in Montreal was David Fennario's *Balconville* in 1979. In this play, French and English neighbours have adjoining balconies. Their conversations alternate and overlap, but it is not until a fire threatens both homes that the two families are able to communicate through their two languages, rather than using language as a weapon to insult. One example from *Balconville* of the way language is used occurs when the French-Canadian father's experience of being fired is intensified by the humiliation he feels since both the management and the union staff are Anglophone. The French-Canadian father says: 'Là, je suis allé voir le gars de l'union. Tu sais ce qu'il m'a dit, le gars de l'union? (*I went to see the guy from the union. You know what he said to me, the guy from the union?*) "There's nothing we can do. The company is stopping their operation in Montreal. They're going to relocate it in Taiwan" . . . Taiwan!' (quoted in Hood, 1989/90: 10). In this play, language is used to illustrate international economic realities as well as local concerns, both of which divided rather than united Canada's warring people.

The French language was used to show the minority position of the French characters in a number of other plays. In *Je m'en vais à Régina* (1975), Roger Auger describes the life of a Franco-Manitoban family whose daughter brings home an English-speaking boyfriend. The boyfriend's refusal to adapt to French results in approximately one-third of the dialogue being in English. This experience is a common one for French-speaking Canadians. Another play which deals with this sort of minority reality is Lina Chartrand's *La P'tite Miss Easter Seals* (1988). By a Franco-Ontarian writer, this play describes the journey of a mother, her daughter and her daughter's friend, from Timmins to Toronto. The two girls are interested in English North American pop culture, and this threatens their allegiance to their own language. The mother tries to prevent this, but her efforts only make the girls want to escape their language and culture even more. The girls purposefully speak English when they wish to exclude the mother from the discussion. Here language becomes a generational weapon as well as an economic one, and the aligning of English Canadian and American cultures indicates what speaking English means to a French-speaking audience.

The English-speaking minority in Quebec did not develop a similar series of plays or a critical discourse to support it (although recent critical work is trying to address this gap). One exception to this is *Anglo!*, a long-running review of the early 1980s by Rod Hayward and Allan Nicholls, which commented wryly on Anglophone life in Quebec. However, in 1988, Marianne Ackerman and Clare Schapiro formed Theatre 1774, a company designed to explore the creative exchange between the English and French theatre traditions. Their first production was an imagistic adaptation of poet Ann Diamond's book *A Nun's Diary*. This production, entitled *Echo* (1989), was directed by Lepage but met with hostility in critical circles. Gilles Lamontagne asked in his review in *La Presse* why Quebec's hottest director was working for two Anglophones and accused the company of trying to rob the vitality of Quebec theatre in an attempt to give life to the impoverished English Canadian culture (1990).[8] In 1991, Leonore Lieblein in an article in *Canadian Theatre Review* states how she felt that the country's two theatrical traditions could not hope to stand on equal footing artistically, the result being inevitably the imposition of one community's ideas on the other (1991: 66).

By the 1980s, the intensely nationalist position of the French-Canadian theatre began to change. The work of Quebec companies, like Théâtre Repère and Carbone 14, with their emphasis on movement, imagistic style and the use of many languages, was seen at the time as one way of breaking down linguistic barriers. Wallace describes how the development of this kind of image-based theatre affected the transfer of theatrical productions from Quebec to Ontario:

---

[8] This statement is somewhat ironic now, given the recent criticism of Lepage's work.

Québécois productions that reach Toronto without being
translated into English are primarily imagistic in style, relying on the theatrical languages other than the spoken word
to make their effect. With its emphasis on physical movement and sophisticated aural and visual technology, this
scenographic theatre is much more evolved in Quebec
than it is in English-Canada, where the playwright's script
continues to dominate dramaturgical attitudes and effect
more literary plays. (1990: 39)

Sarah Hood points out in her article on bilingual theatre, that for Lepage
his use of many languages was a function of a conscious shift away from
an emphasis on text for the conveyance of meaning: 'Lepage is as much
aware of the sounds of his work as of the visual elements' (1989/90: 11).

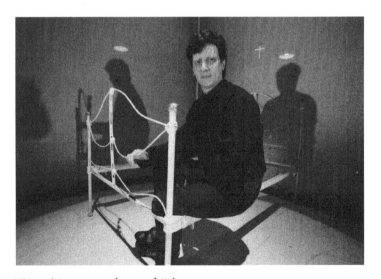

Figure 1 Lepage on the set of *Echo*
Source: Dick Loek / Toronto Star / Getty Images

This movement away from text was easier for Quebec artists than for English Canadian theatre practitioners, since there was less emphasis on the written text for the establishment of a dramatic canon. The use of multiple languages and spectacular scenography soon became the signatures of Lepage's work, signally his desire to speak increasingly to an international audience rather than a local one. Interestingly, he seemed very aware of the limitations of Quebec culture: 'Our traditional reflex of cultural protectionism in Quebec has made us a little xenophobic' (quoted in Dundjerović, 2007: 19). Lepage wanted to challenge the limitations of monolingual theatre in Quebec and the inward-looking approach of Canadian theatre.

While both the English and French theatre communities employed collective creation as a working practice in the 1970s to create nationalist theatre (supporting quite different visions of the nation), in the 1980s, post-nationalist theatre caused a practical divide between the theatre communities of Quebec and English Canada. In Quebec, exploration and experimentation continued even after the swell of nationalism which led up to the 1980 Referendum had subsided, because the reason for employing collective creation was to create new forms, using performance as a metaphor. By contrast, because in English Canada the use of the collectively created performance had as its goal the raising of nationalist consciousness, it fell into disfavour as a working method once the fervour of nationalism had died down. Because in Quebec 'experimentation with theatrical structures and multi-disciplinary forms replaced community research and development as the informing principle of group creation' (Wallace, 1990: 179–80), it continued as a practice, and, in fact, moved towards the mainstream after it was initially introduced. However, in English Canada, once the alternative theatre itself became part of the mainstream, exploration with new forms was dropped in favour of the safety of the literary tradition. While the collective creations of the 1970s in English Canada were very successful, they were an anomaly in the English Canadian tradition which, as a whole, has been predominantly literary in its standards and practices. Ironically, Shakespeare's work increased in popularity in the 1980s in both parts of the country, as an alternative to Molière in Quebec and as a return to safer ground in English Canada.

So while the exuberance of the 1960s and early 1970s allowed for experimentation and freedom to create in both parts of the country, the increased conservatism of the 1980s caused a retreat by English-Canadian theatres to the safety of the literary tradition; meanwhile the theatres in Quebec broke new ground in experimenting with visually oriented non-text-based theatre. Lepage was a leader in this new theatrical adventure. His approach was even heralded as a means of creating a united Canadian theatre. Hunter says:

> Then suddenly, in 1986, a mine exploded at Harbourfront showering fresh sparks of theatrical possibility. Living up to its name, Théâtre Repère, Quebec City's innovative theatre company founded in 1980, set off a series of reverberating signals. *The Dragons' Trilogy* ... was uncompromising in refusing us easy understanding, its juxtaposition of details bizarre and banal, of sensations and arguments, images and silences, exposing painful gaps and illuminating unexpected conjunctions. (1987: 27–8)

This production showed a new approach to appealing to a culturally mixed audience but it was one that had all the hallmarks of Quebec's theatrical traditions of the time.

It is important to point out that the solution to the problem of the country's two languages and cultures could never be entirely addressed by a reduction of the importance of the written text, replacing it with the spoken word. (*The Dragons' Trilogy* is still a play of many words.) In some English communities at this time, there was hostility towards the French language and the nationalist aspirations of Quebec, and this was especially true in the Western provinces, where there was less use for the language. In the French-speaking communities, the reaction to English was equally strong but for a different reason. John Van Burek, former Artistic Director of Théâtre Français de Toronto, says:

> There's wariness as soon as you tell a francophone they're going to see bilingual theatre. For many, bilingualism has

meant well-intentioned anglophones trying to be pan-Canadian. It can be tedious, condescending. French Canadians are very protective about their culture; they have to be. Bilingualism is like the thin end of the wedge. (quoted in Hood, 1989/90: 13)

The issue of language has always been a potent one in Canadian theatre. Therefore, the decision to produce a bilingual production of *Romeo and Juliette* in the late 1980s in the Saskatchewan city of Saskatoon was both contentious and brave. It also speaks to the need for Shakespeare to fill two very different cultural agendas in Canada at the same time.

10 Shakespeare in Quebec

In the context of this bilingual production, it is important to highlight the rise of productions of Shakespeare's plays in translation in Quebec in the late 1980s. During the 1988–89 season, three theatres staged what was called 'l'événement Shakespeare'. This included Lepage's production of *Le songe d'une nuit d'été* at the Théâtre du Nouveau Monde, Omnibus' production of *Richard II*, *Henry IV* (parts I and II) and *Henry V* (the first French-language productions of what was called 'le cycle des rois'), and feminist theatre Espace Go's version of *The Tempest* with a female Prospero. The success of this event surprised even its organisers, with Lepage's production playing to a 98 per cent capacity audience. The reason for this sudden interest in Shakespeare is a question addressed by Marianne Ackerman in an article entitled 'Shakespeare? Oui!': 'As English-language translations of contemporary Quebec plays have often revealed, francophones are much more comfortable with lyricism and poetic flights than are their psychology-bound compatriots in English Canada. Young Quebec artists have found in Shakespeare the density, richness, and freedom of imagination they complain is lacking in most new plays' (1988: 107). The most refreshing thing about these productions by young Quebec artists, she continues, was their freedom both from reverence for the text, instilled in English-speaking actors and directors, and from the political aggressiveness of their Québécois predecessors. She explains:

> Had Omnibus sought to present the same texts even a decade
> ago, Shakespeare's epic tale of how a ragtag English army
> whomped the numerically superior French would surely have
> irritated local nerves. In the charged atmosphere of 1970s
> nationalism, the classics were often forced to address topical
> interests. The poet Michel Garneau's translation of *Macbeth*
> into regional Québécois made it part of the re-examination of
> language and collective identity; the playwright Robert
> Gurik's overly propagandist adaptation, *Hamlet, prince du
> Québec*, recast the Danish court as well-known Canadian
> politicians, and used the play to talk about the perils of
> federalism. But times have changed. Quebec theatre's current
> interest in Shakespeare isn't rooted in politics. (1988: 107)

Ackerman goes on to say that language in Quebec had become an artistic
issue by the 1980s rather than a purely nationalistic concern. Shakespeare's
continued popularity, especially in the hands of young and innovative
directors, could be seen in the fact that Lepage premiered his highly
successful *Le Cycle de Shakespeare* trilogy at the 1992 Festival d'automne
de Paris, where it confirmed his reputation as Brook's heir. In this context, it
is not surprising that the slightly earlier bilingual production of *Romeo and
Juliette*, which sparked national interest in Canada, was largely ignored by
the international critical discourse.

Shakespeare's plays became important to an artistic community that was
open to experimentation and innovation. The fundamental principle of
group creation, which was maintained in Quebec in the 1980s, meant that
the creative process and the creation of a performance were more important
than any literary text, even Shakespeare's text. One of the reasons for
a certain lack of reverence for the literary approach was the fact that the
Québécois language had by and large not been a written one but a spoken
one. Paul Lefèbvre, a Montreal theatre critic, explains: 'The birth of Quebec
theatre resulted from its encounter with speech, after its futile attempts to be
sired by literature' (quoted in Wallace, 1990: 191). But this emphasis on
spoken language does not mean that words were not of value, a point that
Wallace makes clear: 'Words are of extreme importance in this work; but it

is their spoken signification that is of primary interest, not their existence as written text' (1990: 191). Therefore, the rejection of the classical traditions in Quebec, which began with the *refus global*, was the first step in the province's self-determination. A conscious rejection of old models of culture and society was seen as essential for finding new and original forms of expression. The experimentation of the *jeune théâtre* movement was fostered in the 1980s and 1990s by a theatre tradition which laid emphasis on the work of actor/director/créateurs, who replaced the playwright as the instigators of dramatic texts. Lepage has always considered himself a 'global performer', unbound by the conventional divisions of labour in the theatre, and has even likened himself to Shakespeare in this regard. Taking original Québécois translations of Shakespeare to France in 1992 was a way of bringing together a linguistic challenge and a theatrical one.

These translations, of course, came out of a very specific tradition of playwrights whose work contributed significantly to the development of Québécois theatre. The writers responsible for creating the *nouveau théâtre québécois*, including among others Michel Tremblay, Jean-Claude Germain, Jean Barbeau and Serge Sirois (who together helped to establish written forms of Quebec French), brought about a radical shift from the work that went before them. These writers understood the importance to the people of Quebec of making their language heard in front of an audience. For the Québécois, the triumph of Tremblay was, as Wallace says, the acknowledgement that 'the language of Quebec had to be experienced as a public, communal event' (1990: 196). In Quebec, at this time, theatre artists rejected the imposed literary models, replacing them with models of their own making. Claude Des Landes writes:

> Liberated from its dependence on literature and its purely aesthetic pretensions, theatrical expression now relates to pragmatic given facts. ... If authors like Robert Gurik, Michel Tremblay or Jean Barbeau ... have as their major preoccupation to extricate us from the ruts of passivity and colonialism of our history, the present generation, that of collective creation, lets us foresee a utilization of the stage

whose immediate results one cannot be satisfied to evaluate
according to a certain scale. Our entire dramaturgy has just
gone through a first cycle. (quoted and translated by
Usmiani, 1983: 109)

The theatre in Quebec, which began in the 1960s and 1970s by pointing out
the current state of affairs, tried in the 1980s and 1990s to break free of old
patterns to create something entirely new. In many ways, it was a golden
age for Quebec culture, not despite the political problems faced but because
of them.

An engaged debate about the relationship between language and culture,
using Shakespeare's work as a vehicle, is what helped to ignite interest in
Lepage's work abroad. His work was representative of a Québécois theatre
that was moving away from the literary tradition of the playwright working
in isolation, which was redefining the meaning and scope of the *métiers* of
actor, director, designer and playwright. Innovative new theatre companies
in Quebec in the 1980s and 1990s were heartily supported by a provincial
government keen to impress upon the world its unique identity. It is these
companies which gained international attention for Quebec theatre in these
exciting years of expansion and Lepage's approach to collectively created
work and to Shakespeare drew more attention than most.

11 Reflecting on Origins: Lepage's Training and Théâtre Repère

Lepage was born into a working-class family in Quebec City in 1957. His
father was a taxi driver, and his mother was a housewife. But his parents had
spent the Second World War in London, where they both learned fluent
English while his father was in the navy. On their return to Canada, his
parents adopted two children from English Canada. Robert and his sister
Lynda followed. So, the house Lepage grew up in was, from his birth,
a mixture of the country's two official languages and cultures. Having
discovered an aptitude for the theatre, Lepage entered the Conservatoire
d'Art Dramatique de Quebec in 1975. Following his graduation in 1978, he
left for Paris to study with the Swiss director Alain Knapp, along with

fellow Conservatoire graduate Richard Fréchette. The emphasis of the training received was on creating actors who could also write and direct, an approach which helped to form Lepage's concept of what a theatrical artist should be. Another principle developed from his time with Knapp was an idea about imposing limitations on his work:

> J'ai été seulement trois semaines chez Knapp, à Paris, mais un des principes que j'en ai retenu est que plus tu t'imposes des barrières, des limites de temps, d'espace, plus le travail et le spectacle y gagnent; plus le citron est pressé, plus le jus va sortir! Je l'ai toujours cru et j'ai toujours travaillé de cette façon.

> *I was only working with Knapp for three weeks in Paris but one of the principles that I retained is that the more you impose barriers on yourself, limits of time and space, the more the work and the production will gain; the more you press the lemon, the more juice comes from it! I have always believed that and I have always worked in that way.* (Lepage et al., 1987: 179)

After returning to Quebec, Lepage found work with a number of theatre companies, primarily as an actor. He also became actively involved in the Ligue Nationale d'Improvisation (LNI), where he became Recruit of the Year and Star Player par excellence in 1984.

The name and structure of the LNI was designed as a satire of the National Hockey League, by far the most popular source of entertainment in the province. The theatre event emulated the sporting event in every aspect, with a rink for a performing area, an organist who played the national anthem, a referee to hand out penalties and several teams of actors who dressed in hockey sweaters and met regularly for matches during a season which led up to semi-final and final play-off matches. The matches consisted of improvised skits performed by both teams based on subjects which were drawn from a box by the referee. The audience was also invited to participate. Each audience member was supplied with rubber galoshes at the door which could be tossed into the rink as a sign of distaste. The audience was called upon to judge which team had performed best by showing a card that displayed the colour of their favourite team at the end of each skit. Performing in the LNI helped Lepage to develop both his ideas and his talent as what he calls a 'global performer'. So, the ideas Lepage had developed about collective work and individual expression at the Conservatoire, combined with his work in Paris and through the LNI, to develop a creative method, which then began to crystalize when he met Jacques Lessard and began to work at Théâtre Repère.

Lessard established Théâtre Repère in 1980, with a few colleagues and very little in the way of material resources. However, the group produced four shows in the first season which, while they did not have the polish of later productions, already demonstrated the company's themes and pre-occupations. Théâtre Repère was a theatre of research and of unconventional playing spaces. The evocative use of ordinary objects, the primacy of the actor and respect for a research process were all indicative of the company's work. Lessard described the group's work as *'Un théâtre bien identifié à l'âme québécoise'* (a theatre identified with the soul of Quebec; quoted in Beauchamp, 1990: 43). In 1984, Lepage directed his first collectively created piece for Repère called *Circulations*. This production used as its central visual and practical resources a map of the United States and an English language tape, two metaphoric objects used to address Anglophone culture. This show toured successfully across Canada and the United States and drew attention to Lepage's unique vision for the first time. In 1985, Lepage worked with a new group of actors to create the first version of *The Dragons' Trilogy*. He also directed his first one-man show, *Vinci*. Both of Lepage's shows were hugely popular. *The Trilogy*, in particular, received rave reviews and went on to grow in size and scope over the next two decades, touring both nationally and internationally. The enormous success of *The Dragons' Trilogy* established a reputation for Lepage and for Théâtre Repère in Europe for the first time. The striking visual images in the show enabled an international audience to interpret the plays in different ways. The success of these two shows led to further invitations to perform abroad.

When Lepage joined Théâtre Repère in 1982, Lessard research's process was already established. But because of the open nature of this method, Lepage was given the platform he needed to explore his own creative approach. The work that Lepage began to produce with this creative process had a number of common elements. First, it was visually oriented – the spoken text quickly became secondary to the visual one. Also, his work for the Company was filled with both sound and light, which acted to accentuate the transformations of space and time created on stage. The attributes recognised much more recently by Melissa Poll as 'scenographic dramaturgy' were already evident here in his first experiments on stage – straight away physical space took a role in his storytelling. Most importantly for the purposes of this study is the emergence of his recurring themes of travel and the coming together of cultures and the use of multiple languages. Of this, he says: 'All of my works are full of cross-cultural references, languages and different peoples. I'm very interested in artistic dialogue, because it is artistically very rich and challenging and well, interesting. It's not a political statement. I'm interested in exploring people, geography and myth' (quoted in Ackerman, 1990: 15). The universalist stance he takes is clear from this statement and provides the justification for my close analysis of the production process of *The Dragons' Trilogy*. Lepage's interest in feelings over ideas, in myth over politics, is evident in this statement, but I question whether he ever could entirely avoid political engagement in work that deals with the representation of Others and was aimed at presenting Quebec to the world.

Following the initial success of the *Trilogy*, Lepage's career became very busy and for a time increasingly Shakespearean. In 1988, he directed *Le songe d'une nuit d'été* for Théâtre du Nouveau Monde and starred in the Denys Arcand film *Jesus of Montreal* (in which he performs a soliloquy from *Hamlet*). During 1989, he tackled fifteen different projects, including the bilingual production of *Romeo and Juliette* with Saskatoon's Gordon McCall of the Shakespeare on the Saskatchewan Company, which is examined here. In 1989, Lepage was appointed the head of the French Theatre section of the National Arts Centre (NAC) in Ottawa. In 1992, Lepage had the most Shakespearean year of his career, directing a cross-cast production of *Macbeth* at the Graduate Centre for the Study of Drama at the University of Toronto, *A Midsummer Night's Dream* at the National Theatre in London, *The Tempest* at the National Arts Centre in Ottawa and his Shakespearean Cycle that travelled to Paris. This activity resulted in

Video 1 Lepage's early work
Source: The Seven Faces of Robert Lepage, www.youtube.com/watch?v=6nV
AENxMnkw

recognition on the international stage and marked a turning point in his career. From this point forward, Lepage became an internationally sought-after director of opera productions, and his originally created work travelled to theatre festivals internationally, drawing him away from Shakespeare, Canada and the cultural concerns of Quebec, or so it seemed.

12 *The Dragons' Trilogy*

The inclusion here of an extended analysis of the creative process which resulted in Lepage's first internationally acclaimed collective show is intended to highlight the contrast between the working methods used in this environment and his direction of a Shakespeare text. As Fricker says, Lepage is well known now for his 'valorisation of process over product' (2020: 28), and therefore an illumination of his working process seems essential. Not only did this production instigate his theatrical approach; it also established his ideas about representing the 'Other'. Reynolds points out: 'Since his training, Lepage has been committed to an intercultural theatre – which inevitably raises the problematics of representing other cultures' (2019: 67). Reynolds raises the question of why Lepage's work depicted Asian characters but did not, certainly when *The Dragons' Trilogy* was first created, involve actors from Asian backgrounds. To explain this seeming conundrum, I look to the working process that engendered this production.

Like Dundjerović, I see *The Trilogy* as foundational for Lepage, since it established both his creative style and his use of the Repère research approach to create productions that evolved over decades:

> *The Dragons' Trilogy* is an epic production that defined the style of Lepage's theatricality. The story covers most of the twentieth century, three generations, and seven time zones; the production started with open rehearsals and developed into three performance cycles to produce the first version in 1987; and then, into a second version in 2003 – altogether spanning about twenty years. (2007: 75)

Therefore, the first of Lepage's shows to approach head on the idea of cultures coming together was an epic story reaching across three generations that looked at the influence of the Chinese community in Canada. The action of the show moves from East to West within Canada, from the Chinatown in Quebec City (1910–35) to Toronto's Chinatown (1940–55) and finally to Vancouver's Chinatown (1985). The story describes the lives of two cousins, Jeanne and Françoise, growing up in Quebec as children, who slowly discover the cultural world that surrounds them. The presence of the Asian community in Canada has an impact on them at each stage of their lives. In the first piece, or green dragon (each piece is named after one of the dragon pieces in Mah Jong), the two girls play together in the sand, creating the world they know out of shoe boxes. But their world is altered forever when Jeanne becomes pregnant and is staked as part of the winnings in her father's poker game. Her fate is then linked to the Chinese laundry owner (Wong), whose son she is forced to marry.

The girls must suddenly confront their own prejudices about the Chinese family Jeanne has joined.

In a shift of time and place (but not space, as the sandpit stage is the one constant in the production), the friends next find themselves in Toronto. The second section (red dragon), is set during World War II. Jeanne has moved to Toronto after marrying Lee, the son of the laundry owner. Her baby, Stella, has been born with long red hair, indicating her non-Chinese parentage. A pregnant and vivacious Françoise comes to Toronto to visit her cousin on leave from the army. The symbolic use of the stage's properties (the resources that Dundjerović points out are integral to the creative method; see 2007: 75–96) becomes clear during this section when the shoes, which were used playfully in the first part, suddenly indicate the callousness of war, as armed officers crush these remains of individual lives under their feet. Not only does this use of footwear evoke the piles of shoes discovered in the concentration camps, but it acts as a reference to the fact that Jeanne works in a shoe shop in Toronto, serving quite literally at the feet of the English Canadian community. The red dragon illustrates the passions of war through both devastating cruelty and the pain of absence. When Jeanne discovers that she has cancer, she ends her life to avoid facing more pain and sends her daughter Stella to an institution.

In the final section, or white dragon, there is a return to the romantic form, looking to the next generation and art for the resolution of old grudges. Pierre, Françoise's artist son, is living in Vancouver in 1985. He meets a young Japanese woman, Yukali, the granddaughter of a geisha girl and an American officer who were introduced in the Toronto wartime setting (the slippage between Chinese and Japanese cultures and Canadian and American foreign policy is overlooked by the production). The irony of an image of happiness and new life coming out of war stands in stark contrast to the vision of devastation for those on the home front, but the jump in time has healed some wounds. Jeanne is gone, and her silent desperation is punctuated by her daughter's fate; Stella is raped and murdered in the institution she was placed in to protect her. While Fricker aligns the story with Melodrama, I see the intercultural union of two artists as more akin to Shakespeare's romance plays. Pierre has created a representation of the universe which he calls 'Constellation' (encompassing the imagine of the lost Stella). Yukali paints three dragons to represent the soul, providing an image of the individual as a divided being. The performance ends with the coming together of the Western and Eastern cultures and philosophies; the expansive all-encompassing scientific and rational world of the West is married with the philosophy of enlightenment that represents the East. The idealism of this ending has been critiqued by a number of English-speaking critics (Carson, Harvie, Simon, 2000), and this romantic conclusion certainly demonstrates the issue of universalizing human struggles, reducing seventy-five years of conflict to the creation of a beautiful piece of art. However, the sweeping epic tale was embraced by audiences internationally largely, I would suggest, because of its Shakespearean romantic grandeur.

Given that the success of this show resulted in the international invitation which ignited Lepage's career, it is instructive to look at the way this show came into being. Dundjerović writes: '*Trilogy* came about as a result of a year of group research and exploration that took the performers in the direction of the cultural position of the Other, as exemplified through the experience of the Chinese community in Canada' (2007: 77). So, Lepage instigated the idea of working on a cross-cultural piece focusing on the Chinese community in Canada, but the other members of the group were deeply involved in the creative process. The idea of a year-long incubation process was entirely unprecedented in Canadian theatre so this aspect of the creative journey also gained critical attention. So unusual was the show's creative approach that it was documented in detail in *Jeu*, a Quebec French-language theatrical journal.[9] In this volume, Lepage describes how he chose the members of his team:

> Habituellement, une création collective meurt après un mois et demi. La Trilogie est une saga, une fresque. Je voulais qu'elle vive plus longtemps. Ces personnes devaient donc être disponibles et n'avoir entre elles rien de commun, car je ne voulais pas d' 'une gang'. Les gens que je voulais réunir venaient d'horizons différents: certains avaient fait de la radio, d'autres,

[9] This dedicated volume is an example of an approach that celebrates rather than critiques Lepage's intercultural approach to writing in his theatre coming out of Quebec.

du théâtre corporel, de la performance, etc.; mais ce sont des
personnes très mûres et très respectueuses des autres.

*Usually a collective work dies after a month and a half. The
Trilogy is a saga, a fresco. I wanted it to live longer than that.
These people had to be available and had to have nothing in
common, because I didn't want 'a gang'. The people that
I wanted to bring together came from different worlds; some
had done radio, others physical theatre, performance, etc.; but
they were people who were very mature and very respectful of
others.* (Lepage et al., 1987: 180)

This collective way of working is very reminiscent of the characters
featured in the film *Jesus of Montreal* (Arcand, 1989), a film that depicts
a group of actors putting together a radical new interpretation of a mystery
play for the church. The appearance of Richard Fréchette, Lepage's oldest
collaborator and a Théâtre Repère regular, alongside Lepage in a film about
the creative method of a theatre troupe shows how closely reality and fiction
were linked in the Quebec cultural landscape at the time. The inclusion in
that film of two key Shakespearean speeches (one from *Richard III* and
Lepage's delivery of 'to be or not to be') illustrates the idea that while these
young actors were trying to create a new kind of theatre, English, English
Canadian theatre traditions and Shakespeare were all hovering over them.

For Lepage, the assembled company formed the first resource in the
process of creation. But for the story of *The Trilogy*, Lepage also mixed fact
with fiction. Marie Gignac, the actress who played Françoise in the show,
describes how Lepage's instigation of the topic stemmed from a real incident in the life of his family:

Robert Lepage a toujours été fasciné par les Chinatowns.
Sa mère, quand elle était jeune, habitait le quartier Saint-
Roch de Québec, voisin du quartier chinois. Une de ses
amies s'est retrouvée enceinte à l'âge de seize ans, à la fin des
années vingt. Le père de cette amie jouait beaucoup aux cartes
avec un Chinois et lui devait de grosses sommes d'argent. Ce

Chinois désirait se marier; il n'y avait pas beaucoup de Chinoises au Québec, et les mariages entre Québécoises et Chinois n'étaient pas très fréquents. Il a proposé au père de cette amie le pari suivant: 'Si je gagne, j'épouse ta fille et j'efface toutes tes dettes; si je perds, tu n'as plus de dettes.' Il a gagné et épousé cette femme, et ils ont vécu à Québec, heureux semble-t-il. La fille de cette femme, à l'âge de cinq ans, a eu une méningite et elle a du être placée en institution spécialisée à douze ans. Elle y est morte à l'âge de quarante ans, violée et assassinée par un autre patient. Sa mère vit toujours. Cette anecdote très théâtrale et la fascination de Robert pour les Chinatowns constituent le point de départ de la *Trilogie*.

Robert Lepage had always been fascinated by Chinatowns. His mother when she was young lived in the Saint-Roch neighbour-hood of Quebec City, beside the Chinese quarter. One of her friends found she was pregnant at the age of sixteen, at the end of the 1920s. The father of this friend played a lot of cards with a Chinese man and he owed him large sums of money. This Chinese man wanted to get married but there weren't a lot of Chinese people in Quebec and marriages between Quebeckers and Chinese people were not frequent. The man proposed to the father of this friend the following bet: 'If I win, I marry your daughter and wipe out all your debts; if I lose you owe me nothing'. He won and married this woman and they lived in Quebec, seemingly happy. The daughter of this woman, at the age of five, had meningitis and she had to be placed in a specialised institution at the age of twelve. She died there at forty, raped and murdered by another patient. Her mother is still alive. This very theatrical anecdote and the fascination Robert had for Chinatowns constituted the point of departure for the Trilogy. (Gignac in Lepage et al., 1987: 177–8)

Gignac makes it clear that for her the starting point for the show was an anecdote that Lepage recalled and retold to the company. She was motivated by empathy and engagement in this tale in the first instance. So, a bit like Shakespeare, a borrowed narrative thread became another creative resource.

The Trilogy's creative process started, then, with the human resources of the group, an anecdote, and a material resource, a parking lot. Lepage says:

> Le point de départ, en fait, plus que cette anecdote, c'est le parking. Il n'y avait pas de chair autour de cette ressource, mais nous nous sommes vraiment entendus pour partir de ce parking, pour le faire parler, pour l'explorer en surface et en profondeur. Mais pour que nous parlions tous le même langage, pour rallier les gens, les sécuriser dans une aventure aussi vague, je leur ai conté cette petite histoire ... Il s'agissait aussi de confronter deux modes de vie, deux cultures, de considérer à la fois le politique et l'humain.

> *The point of departure, in fact, more than the anecdote, was the parking lot. There was no meat around this resource, but we were very much in agreement to start with this parking lot, make it speak, to explore both its surface and its depths. But in order for us all to be speaking the same language, to bring people together, to make them feel secure in an adventure this vague I told them this little story ... It speaks about the confrontation of two ways of life, two cultures, considering at once the political and the human.* (1987: 178–9)

The implications of a parking lot, which covers over layers of history, has changed for Shakespearean scholars since the discovery of the skeleton of Richard III in Leicester. The fact that DNA samples taken from the skeleton of the hunchbacked king led to a scientific revelation (that his nearest living relative is a Canadian carpenter) reinforces the idea of a connection between a Shakespearean past and a Canadian present. Lepage was already interested in 1985 in what lies beneath the surface of an everyday space like a parking lot and the way history is buried in everyday attitudes and understandings. He also recognised the fact that his 'adventure' was in fact quite 'vague' but exploratory.

The creative process involved in this illustrates how epic storytelling can come about given time and a dedicated company of actors. Gignac describes the first stages of the group's work through her recollection of the way the actors began by exploring their own impressions of China through images. Resources which indicated Asian culture but did not communicate anything specific about individuals or a story were used in this first phase. By considering the pieces of Mah Jong, Chinese cards, and the colours of the Chinese dragons, the group built up a series of impressions. These culturally specific (some have said stereotypical) objects were augmented by objects that each of the actors came up with to contribute to the process. Lorraine Côté brought into the process the shoes which became so evocative of unknown individuals in war. These objects then became scenes through a series of improvisations that aimed to build up a story that spanned twentieth century Canadian history. But the group also needed to ensure that the first phase of the show was sufficiently complex that it could grow and develop over time. The production's story telling is layered and works on several levels to appeal to different audiences in a variety of ways all at once.

Lepage had, from the beginning, the idea of creating an expanding piece, one that could build on the work of the first phase:

> Une heure et demie, trois heures, six heures: l'idée de l'embryon, de la maturité, de l'indépendance. Nous voulions créer trois spectacles autonomes, les produire de façon embryonnaire, trois embryons de spectacle qui ne pourraient survivre indépendamment les uns des autres.

> *One hour and a half, three hours, six hours: the idea of the embryo, of maturity, of independence. We wanted to create three autonomous shows, but produce them in an embryonic fashion, three embryos that could not survive independently from one another.* (1987: 182)

The first phase succeeded in so far as it did what it set out to do. Gignac says of it:

Nous tenions à réussir la première étape, à prouver que cela
était possible: raconter toute l'histoire, montrer qu'elle était
claire, intéressante, et ce de façon elliptique.

*We were determined to make the first stage work, to prove that it was
possible: tell the whole story, so that it was clear, interesting, and to
do it in an elliptical fashion.* (Gignac in Lepage et al., 1987: 183)

The first production of *The Dragons' Trilogy* was only ever performed five
times at the Implanthéâtre in Quebec City in November of 1985 in front of
a small group of spectators.

More improvisational work was done at the beginning of the second stage,
to produce the three-hour version, but this was all focused on the original
outline established in phase one. Lepage says of this process of expansion:

Dans la deuxième étape, nous avions vraiment l'impression
de ne rien inventer, que le spectacle existait par lui-même,
que nous le déterrions. La première étape avait mis en place
toutes les règles. Nous avons laissé grandir le spectacle.

*In the second stage, we really had the impression that we were
not inventing anything, that the show existed on its own, that we
were unearthing it. The first stage had put all the rules into
place. We just let the show grow.* (1987: 184)

Again, it was at the Implanthéâtre in Quebec City that this version had its
premiere. After nine further performances in Quebec, the production moved to
the World Stage Festival in Toronto in May 1986 but was not seen again until
January 1987, when it was performed in Montreal. Performances in Ottawa and
Stony Brook, New York, followed later that year. It was this version of the
show which first toured extensively and was featured at international theatre
festivals,[10] winning prizes and receiving wide critical acclaim.

---

[10] The three-hour version of *The Dragons' Trilogy* has toured to Galway, London,
Limoges (France), Adelaide (Australia), Brussels, Poland, Paris, Amsterdam,

The work developed increasingly and specifically to tour internationally. Even before the second version had completed its initial tour engagements in 1987, work had already begun on the third and final stage, the six-hour version. This version was first performed in Montreal at the Festival de Théâtre des Amériques in June 1987. Marie Michaud, the actress who played Jeanne for the entirety of the initial two-year development process, considers how work on the performance changed when the actors reached the final stage of this improvisational journey:

> Au moment de créer les six heures, les personnages étaient déjà là, on ne les cherchait plus, ils étaient bien campés, précis. En fait, ce sont les personnages qui improvisaient, et c'est d'eux que sortaient les choses.

> *By the time we were creating the six-hour show, the characters were already there, we weren't searching for them anymore; they were well established, precise. In fact, it was the characters themselves who improvised, and it was from them that things emerged.* (Michaud in Lepage et al., 1987: 186)

The opportunity to work with the same character and the same co-creators over a two-year development period was, for the actors in this show, the most rewarding aspect of this adventure.[11] The idea that the characters took on a life of their own, but also that Lepage orchestrated the final form of their expression, is key to understanding this director's approach.

Hamburg, Barcelona, Mexico City, Los Angeles, Boston, Milan, Copenhagen and Jerusalem.

[11] This six-hour production toured to Paris in 1989; Chicago and Los Angeles in 1990; and Switzerland, Milan, Copenhagen, London, Glasgow, Jerusalem, Salzburg, Stockholm and Helsinki in 1991. The show was reworked and remounted in 2003 with a different cast which included two Asian actors. However, this revamped version did not tour nearly as much as the original production with its monocultural cast.

The Dragons' Trilogy was hugely successful, engaging audiences and critics wherever it travelled. There is no doubt that this show was a testament to Lepage and Repère's theatrical creativity and storytelling ability, but was it also a testament to the success of a romantic approach to interculturalism? In thinking about the reception of this production internationally, I pointed out in 2000 that what was seen as a metaphor for the struggles of the people of Quebec inside the nation (the difficulty of being understood when speaking imperfect English) was seen as a real representation of the Chinese community in Canada when this production began to tour to other countries.

> The production that I saw in Toronto was quite obviously an expression of cultural identity by a *québécois* company making themselves heard in Ontario, where their struggle for identity was both familiar and an emotive subject. This was very different from the production I witnessed as an expatriate viewing a generalised image of my home country while living abroad. What I saw as exciting and inspiring in the first context, I found limited and oversimplified in the second. (Carson, 2000: 49)

The fact that the Chinese characters were performed by White French-Canadian actors was not widely discussed in the late 1980s. But in 2000, Jen Harvie also makes the point that '*La Trilogie's* Oriental (and potentially Orientalist) perspective is more apparent than real, . . . the play's focus is more strongly on *québécois* identity than on Oriental culture' (2000: 111). Harvie goes on to point out that the show 'engages nevertheless with Orientalist East/West binary constructions in ways that are productively disruptive' (2000: 111). The willingness of Lepage to take on the stories of others as his to tell was very much in evidence in his early work, and while critical attention was drawn by a range of English speaking critics to the issues of interculturalism it addressed, no critic has to my knowledge drawn specific connections between this production's creative process and this director's relationship to Shakespeare. I put forward here the idea that this sweeping epic tale was received by audiences as part of the romantic tradition of liberal humanism that Shakespeare had come to represent, glossing over the inconsistencies and potential for offence caused by White actors representing Asian characters.

13 Nightcap Productions: Shakespeare on the Saskatchewan

Turning from a collectively created epic piece of theatre to the co-direction of one of Shakespeare's plays in Saskatchewan reveals additional aspects of this director's work and his approach to cross-cultural collaboration. Adding Shakespeare's reputation and position in English Canadian culture into the mix further complicated the issues at stake. The co-direction of a production of Shakespeare's *Romeo and Juliet* raised issues and problems that were both practical and political. While in *The Dragons' Trilogy* the metaphoric Other was discussed and represented on stage by French Canadian actors, in *Romeo and Juliette* a real clash of cultures took place both in the rehearsal hall and on-stage. The shorter English Canadian rehearsal schedule meant that Lepage's company could not approach the play in the same expansive way that *The Trilogy* was created, and the French-speaking actors were forced to abide by rules of a different theatre tradition.

In order to understand the significance of this project and the profound difference in approach to theatrical creation in English Canada it highlights, it is useful to begin with an introduction to the other theatre company involved. Shakespeare on the Saskatchewan began as the summer venture of the co-operative theatre company Nightcap Productions Inc. Gordon McCall, Director of the Summer Festival, was one of the original members of Nightcap Productions and helped spearhead the organisation of this summer venture. Beginning in 1985 with a full-scale version of *A Midsummer Night's Dream* and a second show featuring several famous Shakespearean scenes, known as *Shakespeare's Greatest Hits*, the Shakespeare on the Saskatchewan Festival aimed to present original and accessible productions of canonical texts. Performed in a tent adjacent to the city's Mendel Art Gallery, this company presented the only summer Shakespearean Festival between Vancouver, British Columbia, and Stratford, Ontario.

McCall's productions for the festival were performed in the tent space, and rather than pretending that it was an indoor theatre, the director incorporated the outdoor environment into the show. The company's first production, *A Midsummer Night's Dream*, was set on a golf course because, according to McCall, 'Saskatoon has more golfers per capita than anywhere else in Canada' ('Saskatoon director', 1988: 16). The area under the tent was turned into a putting green, and the audience was asked to sit on blankets around the playing space. For the company's second show, *The Tempest*, the space was transformed into a space-scape and the show was set in the extra-terrestrial future. McCall describes the setting: 'We tunnelled under the ground for Prospero's kingdom and built a small swimming pool in one end of a red shale surfaced playing area' (McCall, 1990: 38). Of *The Tempest*, McCall says: 'This show is geared to be accessible. We won't play down to people. We don't change a word of dialogue' (quoted in Schroeter, 1986: 17). The aim of this Company was to break down the cultural barriers which many of their audience members felt separated them from Shakespeare's work, while retaining the Elizabethan text, a very English Canadian set of aims.

In 1987, the Company tackled the Scottish tragedy, but rather than setting it in the Highlands, set it in Central America to draw parallels between these two locations. Of this choice for *Macbeth*, McCall says: 'We're not trying to stretch the play. . . . The human striving for power can be seen in many contexts, back then, as Shakespeare was writing about it, and right now' (quoted in Bean, 1987: 1). For this show, McCall had a local sculptor build a cement reproduction of a Mayan altar, and the playing space was covered with jungle camouflage. McCall's aim for the Company was to produce commercially viable productions that would appeal to his audiences. McCall says: 'It's finding the metaphorical environment that's right for your audience. . . . You're just viewing one thing through a different set of lenses' (quoted in Bean, 1987: 1). This is not an original justification for changing the setting of Shakespeare's plays (the 1980s performance history is filled with directorial concepts that were created to make the plays more accessible); nevertheless, this approach was used to produce original and innovative productions that appealed to their audiences in this very specific community.[12]

In the company's fourth year, it was able to build on the reputation it had established with a production of *The Taming of the Shrew*, set in Boomtown Saskatchewan, 1903. The set included a railway track which the company arranged to have set down by Canadian Pacific Railway running through the tent and up to a facade of a turn-of-the-century Saskatchewan street: 'Kate was portrayed as a leader of the Temperance movement and Petruchio as an Irish carpetbagger. The character interpretations were based on historical ethnic breakdowns of the community at that time' (McCall, 1993: 3). The highlight of the performance was the entrance of Petruchio on a hand-powered railcar. Therefore each of the productions used an outdoor environmental space which also acted as a central metaphor for the play, not unlike Lepage's own approach to, in Poll's words, 'scenographic dramaturgy'. On the surface, bringing these two directors together made a lot of sense.

The two companies might also have been considered similar in terms of their size financially, although their approach to fundraising was different. In 1987, McCall said of the company's financial record: 'We don't depend on the grants and we will at all costs be fiscally responsible. . . . We open and close the books on each project. So far we've never run a deficit, and I think that's earned us a lot of respect in the business and corporate community' (quoted in 'Saskatoon director', 1988: 16). McCall had set up a company that turned its hand directly to the hard work of fundraising. It was his feeling that if the company wanted to survive in the community, it had to make friends with the community and not take on the role of elite or aloof artists. Lepage's connection to his community was more political than economic; they shared a nationalist outlook. But the divide between the companies was more profound than their approach to fundraising. McCall says: 'I decided I wanted everybody in our theatre to be salespeople. . . . So we did political style campaigning. We went door-to-door and shook everybody's hand. Now we're their friends' (quoted in 'Saskatoon director', 1988: 16). In

---

[12] It is worth pointing out that Lepage directed the same three Shakespeare plays (*A Midsummer Night's Dream*, *Macbeth* and *The Tempest*) in the five-year period from 1988 to 1992.

addition to meeting the community, McCall also made a commitment to serving that community in that he set out to please and satisfy the local audience: 'Saskatoon wants quality theatre and a commitment to the community. ... People here aren't concerned about the national picture and whether a production is going to end up in Toronto' (quoted in 'Saskatoon director', 1988: 16). Therefore, it was to encourage a local audience that McCall approached his theatre productions with both irreverence and enthusiasm. While Lepage was happy to be irreverent about Shakespeare's text, his approach to the art of theatre was somewhat more serious and politically motivated, in the sense that he wanted to bring a Québécois vision of theatre to another part of the country.

For the company's fifth anniversary season, McCall wanted to mount a project that would capitalise on the company's popularity and move towards growth and a wider audience. In addition, the Jeux Canada Games were to take place in Saskatoon in 1989, with special funds being available for projects that related to the games which celebrated Saskatchewan's arts. Both the criteria for this project's funding and the company's five-year objectives included the incorporation of a national component. When McCall realised he could achieve both of these two goals with a single production, he set about planning a bilingual production of a Shakespeare play: 'My idea of "Canadian" component was to produce what I thought would be a truly Canadian collaborative, a bilingual production of a Shakespeare play. ... We entered the competition and were fortunate enough to receive a substantial grant' (1993: 3). McCall contacted Lepage in Quebec City and asked him if he would be interested in collaborating on a piece, possibly *Romeo and Juliet*: 'The primary thought was a collaboration with Lepage. The choice of play would, hopefully, be mutual. As it turned out I discussed *Romeo and Juliet* on the phone. Robert thought this was an excellent choice because it divided into "two solitudes" so well' (1993: 3). Lepage agreed to fly, at his own expense, to Saskatchewan to see *The Taming of the Shrew*. McCall, in turn, flew to Quebec City to see *Vinci* and *The Dragons' Trilogy*. Both directors were impressed by the work they saw and agreed that a collaboration could be artistically challenging. In tackling a cross-cultural production, both companies saw potential advantages, but each approached the role of the artist in society quite differently.

Looking at the way this production process developed, the gap between the English and French-Canadian theatre practices becomes clear. The production, it was agreed, would involve actors from Quebec to play the Capulets and actors from Western Canada to play the Montagues. It was also agreed that the production, while a co-direction, would not be a co-production, and Nightcap Productions would pursue the funding necessary to undertake the expensive project. Administrative support was given by Théâtre Repère, but all the funding was arranged by the Saskatchewan company. The two directors agreed that their *Romeo and Juliette* would be set on a section of the Trans-Canada Highway (TCH), the road which travels the width of the country and connects virtually all of the large centres of population in the Western provinces. A slice of asphalt was specially laid to run through the performance tent for this production to simulate a section of the TCH, and the audience was seated on either side. The 'two-hours traffic' of the stage was literal traffic, as entrances and exits were made in a variety of vehicles, from pickup trucks to old Pontiacs, motorcycles, bicycles, and beds on wheels. The production in Saskatoon was a big success with local audiences who embraced the exuberant style of performance exhibited by both companies, as well as the show's willingness to address the hostilities of cross-cultural communication. Over the seven-week original run of the show, the production played to 95 per cent capacity, with many audience members returning for more than one viewing.

This production then went on tour the following year to four major centres in Ontario: Toronto's World Stage Festival, Ottawa's National Arts Centre, Sudbury, and finally the Stratford Festival. McCall says of the tour: 'The Stratford connection is a most significant development for the Shakespeare on the Saskatchewan Festival. ... We have entered into an agreement with the Stratford Festival to exchange productions, seminars and workshops. This tour is the first stage of this long-term agreement' (quoted in '*Romeo and Juliette*', 1990: 10). McCall's optimism, however, was premature. The tour was greeted with mixed reactions, the most emphatic of which came from the country's two largest papers in Toronto. The two Toronto reviewers both felt that the production choices disregarded the text and that the collaboration failed to produce artistically satisfying results. Robert Crew, writing in the *Toronto Star*, says:

In the prologue of the play, Shakespeare writes of 'the two-hours' traffic of our stage.' I'd hazard a guess that no director has taken this quite so literally before; traffic is everywhere.

The play opens with a beaten-up old Chevy ramming an equally tattered clunker. A couple of pick-up trucks screech in behind them and out pour the good ol' boys in jeans and cowboy boots, slamming and ramming each other into car hoods. . . .

It's all a lot of fun . . . for the first 20 minutes. Unfortunately, the 'two-hours' traffic' is nearer 3 1/2, more than time enough to start wondering where the play itself has gone. (1990)

In *The Globe and Mail* under the headline, 'A Case for the Esthetic Police', Ray Conlogue writes:

The novelty of the *Romeo and Juliette* that opened Monday night at the World Stage Festival at Toronto's Harbourfront is supposedly in its Meech-era collision of two cultures. . . . But the real collision in this production, which reduces it to the esthetic condition of a pair of jalopies after a high speed impact on the Trans-Canada, is the lowbrow/highbrow collision between two directors. (1990)

These two reviews indicate not only how differently the production was received in Toronto but also the extent to which this production demonstrated opposing theatre traditions. These reviews also point out how these critics felt it was their duty to act as the 'Esthetic Police' for the country, an attitude which reveals the extent to which the Western company shared a marginal position with the Quebec theatre artists when being judged by Toronto's cultural elite.

In creating a bilingual production of *Romeo and Juliette*, McCall hoped to 'stimulate a theatrical experience which took the viewer beyond usual preconceptions' (McCall, 1990: 36). Having decided on the concept of a bilingual production of a Shakespeare play, McCall's decision to approach Lepage stemmed from the fact that his work had been compared to Brook, a director whose work McCall greatly admired. In an article in *Canadian Theatre Review* describing the process of creation involved in this production, McCall recalled his first telephone exchange with Lepage: 'I was thrilled at his openness to investigating the possibilities of the project. He demonstrated a strong artistic curiosity for the potential of the undertaking and did not allow political considerations to interfere' (McCall, 1990: 36). Given their combined interest in cross-cultural collaboration, this seemed like a perfect opportunity to explore those ideas. While the initial production in Saskatoon was well received, the tour to Ontario caused tensions between the two theatre companies and their directors. The tour also resulted in the Shakespeare on the Saskatchewan company accumulating its first substantial deficit.

14 *Romeo and Juliette*: 'From Ancient Grudge Break to New Mutiny'[13]

Following the initial phone calls and the visits made to each other's theatres, *Romeo and Juliette* went into preproduction. Co-ordinating schedules across several thousand miles and two languages meant a great deal of administrative work, not least of which was reaching an agreement between the two actors' unions, the Canadian Actors' Equity and Union des Artistes. The budget for this production far exceeded any of the other production budgets raised by a Western company.[14] McCall managed to find financial partners in Festival Saskatoon, the Saskatchewan Arts Board, the City of Saskatoon, the Canada Council, the Department of the Secretary of State of Canada, several national and provincial corporate sponsors, and more than thirty local Saskatoon businesses. In addition to the cost of producing a show in two cities at once, this project also involved a new translation of the parts of the text which would be delivered in French. Lepage took on the responsibility of overseeing this part of the project and negotiated the services of Jean Marc Dalpé, the Franco-Ontarian playwright who had recently received a Governor General's Award

---

[13] Prologue to *Romeo and Juliet*, l. 3.

[14] The budget for this show was $250,000, more than double that of any previous Nightcap Productions show.

for his play *Le Chien*. Dalpé worked towards creating a translation that would recreate the Elizabethan flavour of the language in French and therefore both complement the English text and transcend the regionalisms that divide francophone culture across the country. So, language and its cultural reso-nances were a key component of this production. But for Dundjerović, this was not the main issue:

> However, the show's real importance was not due to its political function, of holding up a mirror to divided Canadian society, but to its creative and collaborative process. In developing the *mise-en-scène* for *Romeo and Juliette*, Lepage explored a long-distance relationship with a company employ-ing another language, with the aim of developing a unified bilingual performance *mise-en-scène*. (2007: 185)

For Dundjerović, this production provided a stepping stone to further collaboration with English speaking companies in other countries. If this is the case, then it is perhaps no wonder that McCall was misled by Lepage's initial enthusiasm for the project. However, the aim of creating a collaborative *mise-en-scène*, through the use of a strip of highway, did provide a new vision of the play.

The two directors agreed at the outset on an overview of the show's intent and outlook. McCall describes this:

> Robert and I had decided that our production would be *Romeo & Juliette* viewed in a contemporary Canadian land-scape/environment. We also hoped to create a production that would offer the audience an experience that we dis-cussed as 'hyper-realism'. We wanted the audience to encounter the action with the immediacy and heightened sense of action that would be created if they were sitting in the middle of a film location set. (1990: 38)

Given both directors' preference for 'scenographic dramaturgy', the Trans-Canada highway seemed an ideal setting; it was iconic in the

Prairie setting but also worked well in terms of the constant movement in the play. McCall describes the importance of this choice from his perspective: 'Our central metaphor became a stretch of highway cutting through a mythical prairie landscape. This ribbon of asphalt was an image of the Trans-Canada highway linking western and eastern Canada, while at the same time it was the town square in Shakespeare's Verona where many of the violent confrontations between the two families take place' (1990: 38). The set was designed to be both evocative and flexible, creating an open space that the actors could populate. The empty space was initially calm, but as soon as the actors made their entrances, the conflict began:

> We viewed the action as a series of violent confrontations –
> the action throughout the play being at a fever pitch:
> intense and violent. The love is as fervent as the hate.
> Romeo and Juliette come together with the violence of
> a head-on collision and are torn asunder with wrenching
> ferocity. The many victims of the play's 'collisions' are left
> on the side of the road like so many road-kills. (McCall,
> 1990: 39)

The metaphor of the road dominated the production's directorial decisions and theatrical style. The sense of a hot summer night when a fight could break out at any minute was palpable. Having real vehicles entering the stage space heightened the sense of danger and realism the two directors were striving for.

According to Dundjerović, 'The emptiness of the space suited the playfulness of Lepage's use of cinematic and theatrical techniques' (2007: 189). Of course, this production predated Baz Luhrmann's famous film *Romeo + Juliet* (1996) by seven years, but its visceral use of objects is quite similar to that adaptation of the play, in which knives and swords are replaced by trucks and guns. 'The objects the directors brought to the stage from real life had, in addition to their kinetic quality, a plurality of meanings' (Dundjerović, 2007: 189). Despite the two directors' stated aim of not using the play to project a political message, the play's casting contained political overtones for its audiences. Given everything that was happening in the country, it was optimistic to believe the production could avoid politics. Lepage says:

> It's also important that people know this is not really about language. You see a bilingual production and immediately you say 'Oh it's about the language issue.' Language is just the skin of culture, not the whole thing. The play is about two different cultures, two different ways of thinking. (quoted in Lacey, 1989: 9)

Similarly, McCall insists:

> While it has obvious connections to our current Canadian dilemma over the Meech Lake Accord plus recent Quebec language legislation, we felt – and feel – that the real conflict in Canada, and in our interpretation of *Romeo & Juliette*, is between cultures and that language differences are the surface reflection of these cultural conflicts. (1990: 39)

Language, then, was used in this production as a symbol of the deeper cultural conflicts between the English- and the French-speaking populations, differences which quickly manifested themselves in the rehearsal process itself.

The two directors worked out a system of co-direction that, on a purely logistic level, worked very well. McCall recalls: 'Before parting that first summer of our meeting, Robert and I agreed on the . . . rehearsal procedure. We would have an eight-week rehearsal period in total. (The longest in our festival's history.)' (1993). The directors had decided from the start which scenes were to be performed in English and which were to be performed in French, based on who was in them and where they took place. As is the case for most French-speaking families in the West (and most immigrant families in Canada), family scenes were performed in their mother tongue, while public scenes were always in the dominant official language, English. The cast was determined collaboratively, through auditions conducted by both directors. The final cast of eighteen members was composed of twelve

Anglophones and six Francophones, a very representative split in terms of Canadian demographics. Most of the French members of the cast had not worked outside Quebec and two spoke virtually no English. The English-speaking actors had as little familiarity with the French language and even less understanding of the Quebec actors' working methods. Thus the cast members represented the experience of two households that this production explored.

Working in two locations with two directors and incompatible rehearsal processes was overcome initially by administrative agreements about how rehearsals would proceed. McCall describes how the rehearsal schedule took shape:

> Rehearsals worked on a staggered schedule. First, Juliette (Céline Bonnier) travelled to Saskatoon in April to rehearse for a week with myself and Romeo (Tom Rooney). Next, Tom and I travelled to Quebec City to work for a week with Céline. Tom stayed on an extra week with Robert and his company but I returned to Saskatoon. Then each company rehearsed their scenes in their home province with their respective directors. Finally, both companies came together in mid-June in Saskatoon to assemble the production with a final two weeks of rehearsal. This final stage of rehearsal was the most challenging, both for the actors and the co-directors. It also proved to be the most exciting of all. (1990: 37)

So, the companies rehearsed separately, except for the two leads, until the last two weeks before the show opened. For this final stage of the process, the Saskatoon rehearsals, the directors also arranged a system of exchange:

> Our system was simple. We had rehearsed the scenes with our separate families before the group came together in Saskatoon. But with all group scenes involving both families, we would work side by side in rehearsal, alternating who

> would do the initial work on the scene. We had agreed upon
> our character and design concept before the joint company
> rehearsal, so we did not run into problems of interpretation.
> Our main job seemed to be getting the characters and scenes
> to where we envisioned them going. Because of the co-
> operative spirit of the company, we were able to accomplish
> this. (McCall, 1990: 39)

While in this comment McCall states that the collaboration was both co-
operative and supportive, it is important to point out that this director
comments on his own words later in the process: 'Please be aware that
I wrote this article immediately following the FIRST production. The
pressures of producing the tour of the production, Robert's fame, and the
tensions surrounding Meech Lake hadn't impacted, as yet. They did the
following season' (McCall, 1993: 1). Both directors have described in later,
more candid interviews, that the experience was less than entirely successful
or co-operative.

Lepage, looking back at the project while in London at the National
Theatre in 1992, said of working with McCall:

> Well, *Romeo and Juliette* was a weird thing because it was
> supposed to be a collaboration, but we were two directors.
> I felt very open to do a lot of things, working with the
> English actors and the French. And I didn't mind the English
> director working with the French actors at all, on the con-
> trary, but he didn't want to. He said that was what we were
> going to do, but in the end he would always be present when
> I worked with the English actors to be sure I didn't contradict
> him. But you have to allow people to contradict your work
> because that's when it thickens and becomes multilayered.
> (Lepage, 1993: 31)

Here Lepage explains a fundamental element of his work which is the
creative energy he finds in contradiction. The clash between the two
directors came about largely due to differing definitions of the role of the

director and contrasting creative processes. When asked in 1992 if he thought co-direction was possible, Lepage replied:

> I think it is possible to have more than one director, but you need to do shows where directing is directing, not imposing. Directing is just finding where the winds are and then positioning yourself to say, 'Well, I think we should go there.' You don't decide where the wind blows, you just try to find out where it is going. And I think one of the problems with *Romeo and Juliette* was that I was ready to do that but the other director wasn't. I thought it was very exciting, the idea of working with both sides, but in the experience I felt cheated. (1993: 31–2)

The theory and practice of cultural collaboration on this occasion became incompatible because of the different working methods but also world-views of the two directors and their acting companies.

Speaking about the hurdles the production faced, Lepage also recounted in 1992 the hostility he felt when French-speaking actors were forced to abide by the English company's rules, largely due to the fact that the Saskatoon company was footing the bill. Working for the first time during this production with the English-Canadian rehearsal system, Lepage was both surprised and frustrated by what he saw as its restrictive nature. Reflecting on the process, he said:

> Well, the two Canadian unions – one French, one English – have entirely different ways of working. Because the French were in the minority, we had to work with the Equity rules, and the French actors didn't like that. The English system is more based on trying to do a show as fast as possible so you don't lose money: so everyone is there all the time for three weeks in a row. But in the French system people are there only when they are called, and you can spread the rehearsal over ten weeks, twelve weeks. (1993: 32)

In his frustration with the system's pragmatic efficiency, Lepage was reported to have said to the executive director of the Professional Association of Canadian Theatres, Catherine Smalley, during the rehearsal of *Romeo and Juliette:* 'You know you're not making shoes; you're making theatre' (quoted in Godfrey, 1991). While the French actors were frustrated by the imposition of the English way of doing things and the pressure which money seemed to place on artistic decisions, it is important to point out that the actors were being supported by funds that had been raised by the Western company in an agreed-upon rehearsal schedule.

Much more recently the distinctive approach taken by Lepage in rehearsal has been described by Reynolds: 'contradiction is not an abstract principle, but a functioning creative principle which drives Lepage's process' (2019: 19). McCall experienced this aspect of Lepage's direction with some frustration:

> I feel that Robert attempts to create anarchy within a group. He indicates that creativity is generated by it. I believe he felt our process was far too organized and harmonious. ... I found Robert's work to be frequently instinctually brilliant but I feel instinct, which also informs my own work, must be accompanied by sound justification back to the text. Robert never liked these discussions because he doesn't want to be restrained, as he sees it, by justifying his choices. This is fine given unlimited budgets and rehearsal time and the opportunity to bring projects back to life several times in an ongoing investigation. We did not have that luxury with the circumstances surrounding *Romeo and Juliette*. (1993: 6–7)

Reynolds identifies the tendency to cause disruption as a key element of Lepage's approach: 'Lepage, then is the troublemaker par excellence – creating problems for others to sink their teeth into' (2019: 19). McCall was frustrated by the practical restrictions presented by working in this way when time and money were short, but he also indicates a very English Canadian approach to Shakespeare interpretation, in that he felt all of his artistic choices needed to be justified by the text – something Lepage found entirely unnecessary.

McCall's initial public response to the collaboration in his article in *Canadian Theatre Review* was diplomatic:

> We both learned from one another throughout the process and as theatre practitioners, I believe we both gained significantly. From a cultural standpoint, I was not as aware of culture influences affecting our work. Only an outside observer could make a proper judgement on that aspect of our partnership. On the other hand, we both agreed that our communication was eased by our mutual fluency in the language of theatre. Because our directorial influences had certain similarities, this situation was made easier. (1990: 40)

After the tour of the production to Ontario, which resulted in the Western Company's deficit, McCall felt angrier about the experience and the critical response it received. McCall felt his contribution to the show was not properly acknowledged. McCall's central reason for disappointment might be seen in his conclusion to the *Canadian Theatre Review* article. In it, McCall makes plain the fact that he saw the project in terms of further possibilities for Canadian theatre. He concludes:

> The benefits of this kind of experience to our national cultural community, particularly our theatre community, are immeasurable. This project has allowed cultural and theatrical influences to affect the work of two groups of artists who might never have come into contact. The effects have all been positive. It seems to me that we have everything to gain and nothing to lose by proceeding further in this direction. ... Perhaps we do not need to produce works of literal political messages but rather collaborative efforts that show the willingness and ingenuity of Canadians already speaking a common language: the artists. (1990: 41)

Lepage, on the other hand, viewed the show in more personal terms: 'I thought it was very exciting, the idea of working with both sides, but in the experience I felt cheated' (1993: 31–2). McCall's response shows both optimism and a sense of ownership of the larger (political) goal of creating Canadian culture. Lepage saw the show more as part of his own creative voyage of discovery and, according to Dundjerović, a trial run for his next project, a collaboration with Scottish actors on *Tectonic Plates* (2007: 185). What was set up as an attempt to bridge the gap between artists to create something truly Canadian resulted in an experience of miscommunication. Rather than breaking down barriers, this collaborative process reinforced them. However, both companies were forced to experience and recognise the contexts which had created two quite different artistic cultures, with divergent aims as well as practical rehearsal processes.

15 A Critical Analysis of Early Multicultural Government Policy in Canada

The failure of this project to create a harmonious piece of pan-Canadian theatre raises questions about the expectations underpinning the belief that such a venture might be possible. While putting in place multicultural policies expressed the good intentions of government ministries and arts councils, the successful application of those policies must be questioned. The reaction of minority groups to multicultural policies, which can be patronising or encourage ghettoisation, is often a sense of dissatisfaction and frustration. A brief introduction to the debates which surrounded multiculturalism in the theatre can usefully begin with a critique of the ideals of the governmental multicultural policies that were in play at the time when these projects were conceived. The ideas which Howard expresses more recently about 'antiblackness' are an echo of the anger felt in this earlier period by a range of cultural communities in Canada in the late 1980s and early 1990s.

Multiculturalism in English Canada was encouraged through government policy and, as such, was often seen as a means of disseminating power from above. In Quebec, the preference was always for the term interculturalism. Howard explains the reason for this difference in approach:

> Quebec claims interculturalism rather than multiculturalism. Though more a difference in nomenclature than policy, Quebec insists on interculturalism in the context of its own nationalist struggle within Canada, which, not without some justification, rejects the strategic mobilization of multiculturalism by the government of Canadian Prime Minister Pierre Trudeau to discipline the province's claims upon it (Nugent). Yet within the province, this distinction frames the particular hierarchical relationships between a white Québécois Francophone majority – *les Québécois de souche*[15] – and what it refers to as its 'cultural communities.' (2020: 127–8)

Quebec has assumed a sense of solidarity with its 'cultural communities' because of its own minority position within Canada. But this presumption of solidarity through marginalisation results in the erasure of difference that Howard identifies.

Canada became officially bilingual and bicultural from the instigation of the Royal Commission on Bilingualism and Biculturalism in 1963. The complexity of speaking about multiculturalism as a national policy becomes clear when thinking through the implications of representation. Inevitably being a member of a dominant group of any kind, in a position of power, makes it difficult to critique the hierarchy of which one is a part. As a Westerner, McCall felt no sense of power or pre-eminence when staging Shakespeare, but as an Anglophone, from Lepage's point of view, there was a clear linguistic hierarchy in place. As an adaptation of nationalist rhetoric, multiculturalist rhetoric can be seen as a continuation of colonial ideals, taking ethnicity and formulating it into manageable representative packages

---

[15] Un Québécois de souche est un peu l'équivalent québécois des descendants des W.A.S.P. (white anglo-saxon protestant) américains. (A *Québécois de souche* is sort of the equivalent of the W.A.S.P. Americans; Louys, 2018.)

which can be demonstrated and displayed as folkloric spectacle. In order to create real multiculturalism, or interculturalism, a confrontation must take place with the established institutions. Looking at the production of *Romeo and Juliette* in this light, the fact that it was specifically funded to add a national element to an event taking place in Saskatchewan immediately put the French actors at a disadvantage. The imposition of the work of Shakespeare also favoured the English actors' textual tradition. So, the power stayed firmly with the English-speaking company both financially and artistically in this case, despite McCall's protestations.

16 Quebec's Multiculturalism/Interculturalism

To understand multiculturalism in action in Canada in this period, it is worthwhile to examine the differing definitions and interpretations of federal multicultural policy in Quebec and the rest of the country. Quebec is a very particular case in terms both of its experience and its practice of setting up relationships with immigrant communities. The majority in the province, the Francophone population, had at this time gained political power relatively recently, only since the Quiet Revolution and the rise of the separatist Parti Québécois. That process of empowerment was achieved, to some extent, at the expense of the other minority groups in that province, the largest and most worrying of which, for the French, was the English-speaking minority. Not only did this group present the largest threat linguistically to the survival of North America's only French-speaking community, but it was also perceived as being responsible for the slowness of the dissemination of power to the people of Quebec. In order to combat the seeming sea of English influences, Francophone Quebec passed a number of very strict language laws, the most controversial of which, Bill 101, forbade English signs on storefronts throughout the province (among other measures), to support the French language culture and suppress the influence of the English language. Fricker articulates this:

> The Charter of the French Language or Bill 101, which the
> sovereigntist Parti Québécois enacted a year after it took
> power in 1976, requires immigrants to send their children to

> French-language schools, businesses with more than fifty
> employees to be run in French, and commercial signs to be
> in French. (2020: 40)

The efforts of the Quebec government to maintain, and in fact increase, the
Francophone population, despite a threateningly low birth rate, necessitated
control over both immigration and the integration of newcomers into
Quebec society.

> While the other Canadian provinces have since developed
> their own immigration policies, Québec remains the pro-
> vince with the most control over selecting and educating its
> immigrants. Assuring that French remains the only official
> language of the province and the language of common usage
> has been one of the most controversial aspects of Québec
> government policy. (Fricker, 2020: 40)

Quebec society changed once the political power was in the hands of a party
whose aim it was to deliver sovereignty, with the powerful slogan 'Maîtres
Chez Nous'.

The basis of Quebec's official policy regarding cultural communities was
established in 1978 by a White Paper entitled 'La Politique Québécoise du
développement culturel'. Ines Molinaro outlines the main goals of this paper
in the following way:

> The main objectives as delineated in these policy state-
> ments include the assurance of the maintenance and devel-
> opment of cultural communities and their uniqueness; to
> inform and sensitize francophone Quebec about the con-
> nection between the cultural communities and the com-
> mon cultural heritage of all Quebec inhabitants; to
> encourage the integration of the cultural communities
> into Quebec society, and especially in sectors where they
> are presently under-represented, particularly in the public
> service. (1992: 4)

As Molinaro points out at the time, these policies were in line with the Federal policies of the Ministry of Multiculturalism, but she goes on to say that in their execution these policies were not as open as they seemed. The government's policy of equal employment in the civil service was not as fair as it might have been, since this policy was announced at a time when employment opportunities in the government were disappearing. As a result of these events, the Montreal schools, as the place where the largest number of mixed groups would meet, became the centre of multicultural activity in the province.

But the increasing diversity of the community in Montreal created a divide between the urban and rural populations of Quebec and their differing visions of the Province. Even the word *Québécois* was variously used to describe both the French-speaking majority and any member of the new community of Quebec. As a result, the more precise terms Howard uses were developed to describe these two different groups; '*Québécois de souche*', referring to the old stock francophone population, and '*néo-québécois*', referring to the more recent arrivals. Because the success of Quebec's bids for nationhood rested on an idea of nationalism which required a unity of spirit, if not of origin, the constitutional negotiations of the early 1990s settled on describing the province as a 'distinct society'. Nationalist rhetoric of any kind, however, was hard-pressed to accommodate the increasing heterogeneity of the Province's urban centres. Howard makes this point in 2020, specifically in terms of the arts in Quebec in general and Lepage's work specifically. He writes:

> Within this context driven by the self-interest of the hegemonic Quebec nationalist project, Black people are forced to choose between, on the one hand, cooperating with Quebec antiblack-ness in order to gain a toehold on inclusion in the community, and on the other hand, naming and resisting antiblackness and being relegated to outsider status. (2020: 132)

Again, what Howard applies to racial difference in 2020 I want to highlight in terms of language identity in the past. Fricker makes a key point when she writes:

> Many Anglophones saw the Bill as a hindrance to their
> liberties and left the province after it was passed, but it has
> remained policy ever since and is regarded by many to have
> played a central role in keeping French the majority lan-
> guage in Québec. (2020: 40)

So language laws, immigration policy and other ways of creating and sustaining a sense of national pride in Quebec were established in the 1970s, but these structures have not been altered since, despite the fact that they may no longer be fit for purpose.

In the late 1980s and early 1990s, conflicts also arose in the province with the Indigenous population in terms of land claims and self-determination. These debates placed the First Nations people in the middle of a jurisdictional dispute between Canada and Quebec over control of land and resources, rendering questionable the claims of cultural 'authenticity' (meaning originality but also authority) used by Quebec. In the face of a declining birth rate, many Francophones favoured protective action in the form of birth incentives and asymmetrical immigration policies to promote their culture. But, not surprisingly, problems arose. Since the waves of immigration to Quebec in the 1980s were predominantly from Indochina, Latin America and South Asia, what Howard calls Quebec's 'antiblackness' created issues of racism for anyone who did not appear to be of European origin or who was indifferent to the Province's collective project. Visible minorities experienced racial prejudice and discrimination if they refused inclusion in the Québécois vison of community, and as Howard makes clear, these communities worried that their concerns were of little impor-tance in a provincial government which was more interested in procuring powers from the federal government that would help preserve the dom-inance of the Francophone majority.

The central problem that faced Quebec at the beginning of the 1990s was one of numbers: a declining Francophone majority, an ageing population and a dwindling English-speaking community. The disintegration of the English-speaking community, due to a rise in emigration from the province by young mobile English-speaking Québécois, was only perceived as a danger to the fabric of Quebec society after they had gone. This acknowledgement of the importance of the influence culturally of the English-speaking community in Quebec was very new and signalled a change in attitudes. While it is impossible to give an exhaustive account of the complex issues being addressed in the province at the time, this overview draws attention to some of the key points of concern regarding multicultural policy as it relates to the language debate in Quebec. Howard concludes his much more recent assessment in the following way: 'True justice will require an even more radical upheaval. It will require the arts in Quebec, the Quebec state, and the Québécois people more broadly to consider the kind of identity they want to claim' (2020: 143). Therefore, the problem of representation and cultural identity for Quebec's 'cultural communities' remains a live issue which cannot be summed up simply through a bilateral relationship between language and culture.

17 English Canada's Approach to Multicultural Policy

The notion that English Canada had a more plural view of society is also debatable. Janice Kulyk Keefer examines English Canadian literature as a means of discussing the relationship between culture and society's changing perception of itself (1992). She cites the changing nature of Canadian literature as an example of the shift which was taking place from a canon dominated by Anglo-centric views, to one which accepted hyphenated Canadians on their own terms. To replace the dialogue which had dominated the country's cultural history previously, the battle between English and French, she highlighted the need for a polylogue, a creative manifestation of the government's multicultural policy, but one which was generated from the ground up rather than from a policy level downwards.

In the introduction to *Other Solitudes*, Linda Hutcheon points out how the ideal vision of multiculturalism is often a long way from reality; 'Views of the stereotyping and ghettoizing tendencies inherent in multicultural policy and its implementation are testaments to the power of fear, ignorance, and prejudice that even the most idealistic of ideologies cannot eradicate' (quoted in Kulyk Keefer, 1992: 26). Kulyk Keefer stresses the need to recognise English, Irish and Scottish origins as ethnic origins like all others in Canada, and not as the norm against which other experiences must be compared.

Kulyk Keefer saw at the time the need for oppressed groups to throw verbal stones at the dominant group and their hierarchies and institutions in order to redress the balance of power. While some writers in the early 1990s wanted to write specifically for their community, others wanted to write for the Canadian community at large. As in Quebec, transcultural writers in the rest of Canada were challenging the expectations and criteria set down by federal policies, or as Kulyk Keefer puts it, 'the code of "good behaviour" demanded by the Department of Multiculturalism, a code which . . . demands that "multicults" sing pretty songs and not make shrill demands for access to political power' (1992: 25–6). In Canada in the late 1980s and early 1990s, there was a growing divide between ethnicity and race, ideology and reality, and the theatres were central in trying to grapple with these issues.

Introducing an issue of *Canadian Theatre Review* dedicated to Theatre and Ethnicity, Carol Off describes the situation during this decade in the theatre in relationship to the funding of multicultural projects. She cites the fact that all ten provinces had either a Multicultural Theatre Association or a provincial organisation that embraced multiculturalism, as evidence of the positive effects of government funding to this area. She does not claim, however, that it was an unmitigated success:

> It's all creating a new vitality in the ethnic arts communities. But it's also creating confusion and ambiguity in the definitions of multicultural arts (even among its practitioners); it's questioning the way the ethnic arts are funded, and it's cast aspersions on the government agencies responsible for funding them. (Off, 1988: 6)

There were certainly those at the time who saw government funding of multicultural theatre as promoting ghettoization. Ironically when Lepage began to tour his intercultural theatre abroad, he managed to avoid, in part, local critical assessment of his inter/multi/transcultural credentials. While battles about these issues raged at home, his work was warmly embraced at theatre festivals worldwide.

Turning back to the two case studies under examination, one question that might be asked is what relationship developed between the creative method used and the power structures which emerged in the execution of the creative process. In *The Dragons' Trilogy*, the creative method chosen was collective creation, yet within that, there was a creative research process that was imposed. The research approach of Théâtre Repère and Lepage's direction controlled the outcome, even if the outcome was fluid over time. The make-up of the group was also entirely determined by Lepage. In *Romeo and Juliette*, the production involved a co-direction, but how did that decision actually effect the work which took place when the two companies came in contact? The idea of Lepage as the coordinator of the ideas of others, rather than a director in the sense of the European autocratic auteur, was accepted practice within Quebec, when he was working with others who were familiar with the theatre-making methods of his company. However, once this director began to work outside his home province and beyond the country's borders misconceptions about his approach to the role of the director became more common. The link with Brook was just one element of this misconception of his approach. Arriving in London in 1992 to work with a group of English actors at the National Theatre also resulted in misunderstandings. Lepage said at the time:

> There is a sense of respect for the director in British theatre that I am discovering, and, well, it's a nuisance. Everyone is so at your disposal – and that's English Canadian as well. They're disciplined, they are there on time, and they listen to what the director wants, and they do it. (1992: 32)

Lepage's position as the conductor at the centre of a creative symphony in Quebec was challenged when faced with English and English Canadian actors who expected instruction. Therefore, in Canada in the late 1980s and early 1990s, there was a complex debate circulating about inter/multi/ trans/ cross-cultural issues. Lepage's work managed to avoid controversy in the press at the time by appealing to Quebec's vision of a nationalist theatre of self-definition and English-Canada's ideal of a multilingual, metaphoric theatre that could be pan-Canadian. But some of the critical work of this moment foreshadowed what was to come.

18 The Cultural Controversy of 2018 Revisited

The creation of his own theatre and workshop spaces in Quebec City (Le Caserne Dalhousie in 1994 and Le Diamant in 2019) established for Lepage and his company Ex Machina an environment that was developed with his creative method in mind. These two laboratory spaces helped develop some of the most extraordinary and technically complex theatrical creations of the twenty-first century. They have also helped consolidate Lepage's working methods and creative partnerships. The combination of a close-knit group of artists and a familiar environment has created productivity on an industrial scale, as Ex Machina regularly exported several productions a year to other parts of the world. Large cultural organisations like the Metropolitan Opera Company and the Stratford Festival have bowed to Lepage's way of working, giving the impression of an almost unstoppable central creative force. His home base was where Lepage was both understood and valued. However, the controversy which arose because of the two productions which caused offence due to cultural appropriation saw the dismantling of key collaborations in 2018.

SLĀV enraged the Black Francophone community in Quebec, while *Kanata* united the Indigenous artists of Canada in protest, resulting in the first serious backlash to this director's work outside the relatively polite circles of theatre criticism. The focus of the controversy on this occasion was specifically the issues of cultural imperialism and appropriation and much of the debate took place online, on Twitter and Facebook. Given the approach taken from the start of Lepage's career to other cultural groups he has represented, it seems odd that a cultural analysis of this director's work did not feature before in the popular press. However, as this analysis indicates, in the past Lepage and his co-creators from Quebec felt they were in a marginal position, their voices oppressed, especially when working on Shakespeare in English Canada. But was this really the case, even in the 1980s? Now that Lepage has attained international status, incredible power lies in his hands to dominate or exploit Others through his presentation of their stories. One might imagine that his early experiences in Saskatchewan might have made him sensitive to this shift in his current position. But his overarching belief in the freedom of the artist, and the empathetic approach of Quebec's inter-culturalism, has given Lepage a sense of exceptionalism.

As a means of concluding this exploration of Lepage's early work, I want to return to the 2018 controversy to raise the question that Lepage puts to his critics: Do artists have the right to offend in the name of freedom of expression? The *Huffington Post Canada* ran a story under the headline 'Robert Lepage's *SLĀV*, a Play with a Mostly White Cast Singing Slave Songs, to Run across Quebec' (Valiante, 2018). Giuseppe Valiante's article was quickly updated to include the following correction: 'Montreal's jazz festival cancelled the show's run in July'. Less than a month later, *The Guardian* ran an article about the second problematic performance Lepage was involved in; 'Robert Lepage has scrapped a controversial production accused of appropriating indigenous history, marking the second time this month the Canadian has come under fire for his portrayal of non-whites' (Kassam, 2018). This article goes on to highlight the meeting between Mnouchkine, Lepage and the Indigenous artists and points out that the result was not greater understanding but rather a decision to cancel the project due to what Lepage calls 'the infinitely complex and often aggressive controversy surrounding the show' (quoted in Kassam, 2018). The arguments of the Indigenous artists were impossible to reconcile with Lepage's stance on artistic freedom. Perhaps this is why the production was performed in a revised version in France where the rights of the artist were seen as of paramount importance and this issue became the focus of the show.

In Lepage's statement on Facebook about *SLĀV*'s reception, he denounces the intolerant comments that were made in the street and on social media. He speaks of the freedoms that he feels have been taken away because of this experience:

> To me, what is most appalling is the intolerant discourse heard both on the street and in some media. Everything that led to this cancellation is a direct blow to artistic freedom, and after 40 years of working in the theatre, I think I can legitimately address this part of the question. (Lepage, 2018)

What interests me in the context of this examination of his early work is the fact that Lepage claims to be an innovator in this area and a defender of the rights of minority groups. The statement goes on:

> Over the course of my career, I have devoted entire shows
> to denouncing injustices done throughout history to specific
> cultural groups, without actors from said groups.
>
>   These shows have been performed all over the world, in
> front of very diverse audiences, without anyone accusing me
> of cultural appropriation, let alone of racism. Quite the
> contrary. These projects have always been very well
> received and have contributed to make Ex Machina one of
> the most respected theatre companies in the world. (2018)

Of course, Lepage ignores the critical discourse instigated by Anglophone critics I have cited here. Howard points out how the Quebec press and artists often discount Anglophone approaches because it is assumed that they are hostile to Quebec's nationalist project. This assumption influenced the perception of where the criticism of SLĀV was coming from in Montreal:

> Ultimately, the media and public discourse considered the
> resistance to be coming chiefly from those who do not
> understand Quebec, indeed who are perhaps not from
> Quebec: those who are Anglophone, influenced by
> Anglophones, or influenced by ostensibly irrelevant critical
> discourses that are 'marked by the Anglophone context'.
> (Howard, 2020: 140–1)

Howard points out that 'while the resistance to SLĀV was homegrown and led by Francophone Black people, it was presumed to be coming from hostile Anglophones' (2020: 141). This might be seen as 'antianglophoneness' which, similar to 'antiblackness', dismisses through antipathy, rather than empathy in this case, the voices of individual critics who happen to speak English. But this examination makes it clear that language alone is not a determinant of culture and viewpoint.

   When I questioned Lepage in 1992 on the topic of cultural appropriation in *The Dragons' Trilogy*, he admitted that if the roles were reversed, he would not respond well:

> Every Chinese person we met . . . said it was moving, it was
> extraordinary and we laughed so much when they were
> trying to speak Chinese. . . . I would be offended if I saw
> someone doing a French-Canadian character and they didn't
> have the right accent but that's a cultural attitude. The
> Chinese don't have that problem at all. (1993: 34)

Rather than being surprised by the controversy which arose in the summer of 2018, I am somewhat surprised that it has taken so long for the intercultural credentials of these productions to be examined publicly. Positioning himself as an apolitical member of a thwarted and ignored subculture, Lepage has managed to avoid this kind of scrutiny for a very long time. But when faced with the anger of members of the Quebec Francophone community in a discussion about *SLĀV*, Lepage was taken by surprise:

> I was warned by some people that I was probably going to be
> dealing with a band of 'radicalized Anglos from Concordia
> University,' my whole argument was prepared in English.
> But when I realized that the vast majority of them were
> francophones and that the discussion was going to take
> place mainly in the language of Molière [French], I must
> admit that I found myself at a loss for words. (quoted and
> translated by Howard from Boisvert-Magnen, 2020: 141)

Not only does this illustrate Lepage's inability to accept homegrown criticism; it also points out his own split personality, making a different argument in English and in French, assuming that his audience is not like him (and ostensibly the country) both bi/multi-lingual and bi/multi-cultural, and therefore capable of a variety of outlooks and opinions.

This argument does not attempt to undermine the work of this director; it is rather a suggestion that this reckoning was due. Lepage attained celebrity by association due in part to comparisons with Brook. By heralding the rights of the artist over the rights of members of the cultural groups he represents, Lepage has taken a stance which is now considered part of an outdated earlier creative approach, multiculturalism. Moving from the

margins to the centre of theatrical creation worldwide has brought increased
scrutiny and responsibility. The exposure to critiques from around the
world and through social media has created an environment of increased
resistance for projects like those undertaken by Lepage. Many of the
comments responding to his statement published on Facebook are clearly
by people who have not seen the show in question, which raises again my
point (and his) about informed debate. It is a shame that just when the
majority of the population has a voice, it seems that a dialogue is not
possible. In his statement, Lepage says:

> It's obvious that any new show comes with its share of
> blunders, misfires and bad choices. But unlike a number of
> other art forms theatre is not fixed. It's a living art form, that
> allows a play to grow and evolve constantly, to be perpe-
> tually rewritten according to audience reactions, and to be
> fine tuned show after show. (Lepage, 2018)

In the recent past, Lepage's productions have shifted and changed in response
not just to audiences but to critical assessments, what Poll calls 'auto-
adaptation' (2018). *The Trilogy* was recast with Asian actors in 2003,
Needles and Opium was reworked and remounted in 2013 to tour, and the
revised production featured the black dancer Wellesley Robertson III in the
(silent) role of Miles Davis (rather than this role being played, as it was
originally, by Lepage himself). Adjustments have been made, but to truly
involve a wider audience in the dialogue that these productions undertake, it
seems that Lepage may need to open his creative process to a wider group of
participants, both on and off the stage, inside and outside the theatre. Perhaps
Lepage's work has not really been exposed to as wide an audience as he might
have imagined, given that the theatre audience continues to be mainly White,
educated, middle-aged and middle class (see Video 2 for an explanation of the
Ex Machina creative process). The stance he took in 2018, as misunderstood,
does not acknowledge the fact that the accommodations he has made to his
casts (including Asian actors in the casts of both the *Dragons' Trilogy* and
Seven Streams of the River Ota) could be seen as tokenism. Fricker points out
how the adjustments to the original may not have achieved the desired aim:

Video 2 Robert Lepage: Creating outside of the frame
Source: www.youtube.com/watch?v=pMGPzuF7B_Q

'the casting of one English and two Asian actors to play the foreign roles (the original cast were all white Quebecers) feels like a misstep: It makes literal and seems to sanction what the production seems otherwise at great pains to point out are externalized, distant impressions of otherness' (2003). Even critics who want to continue to support his work have had trouble doing so when viewing a reaction to criticism which involves abandoning his metaphoric approach. Altering productions which are twenty-five to thirty years old creates new problems. The kind of quiet ongoing dialogue that Lepage has developed with worldwide elite audiences and theatre critics may no longer be possible in a post-pandemic world. The future of experimental theatre will need to consider how to include an audience of a younger, more social media savvy generation of multilingual and intercultural individuals into its concerns if it is to avoid the kind of reaction the 2018 productions received. Lepage needs to return to his point of origin in his directorial work, as he has done in his solo creations. His most recent solo show *887* details his childhood in Quebec City and the multicultural upbringing that led him to want to speak to a range of audiences through a variety of languages, both verbal and visual. His success so far has been based on allowing his audiences (and he does now have a global following) to interpret his ideas as they see fit, feeding their responses into evolving epic productions. If this dialogue breaks down, then it will be the end of this kind of exciting experiment and the world of theatre will be a darker place for that. But it is equally essential that this director, like other internationally renowned artists, acknowledge and accept the responsibility that comes with the fame and position of influence his work has acquired. Little has changed in Lepage's work over three decades, but his potential theatre audience is radically different.

The celebrated artist Lepage has become cannot excuse his universalist approach to the presentation of the stories of Others on the basis of artistic freedom. *The Dragons' Trilogy* has been accused of Orientalism, although Lepage counters this with his vision of the show as an exposé of clichés over time. In 1992, he stated:

> I think that *The Dragons' Trilogy* is an interesting example of our vision of other cultures. The first part gives us a very clichéd vision of what the Chinese are, but that's the vision we have of the past. I wasn't there in 1925, but what our parents transmitted to us in Quebec City was that vision, that's how they told the story. The second section is a bit more accurate, but still we weren't close friends with the Japanese during the Second World War. We saw documentaries about the war, but we can't really know what motivated them, although it is much closer. But the Japanese girl in the art gallery in the last section we know very well: she's not a cliché, she exists. So I think it is a good example of how the relationship between these two cultures, the Canadian culture and the Asian culture, has evolved. (1993: 34)

The fact that Lepage elides the Chinese and Japanese cultures under the general umbrella of Asian culture is telling. *The Trilogy* begins with the Quebec characters saying the line 'I have never been to China' (in three languages). That is no longer true for this director or for his audiences. The world has become a smaller place through the familiarity generated by the

Internet and international travel. Examining clichés can be a way of exhibiting and reinforcing them. If Lepage's work is to avoid the kind of controversy he faced recently, he might consider revisiting his own early work on cross-cultural collaboration within Canada. As Lepage admitted himself in the online interview which accompanied the broadcast of *Coriolanus*, following the pandemic, theatre makers will need to start over (2020b).

The time is ripe for a *Dragons' Trilogy* that engages with the real Chinese community in Canada in a significant way, or a *Romeo and Juliette* that shares the burdens of finance and explores the practical hurdles of working with the two performance traditions in the country. It seems extraordinary that Lepage has instead mounted a world tour of his *Seven Streams of the River Ota*, which considers the impact of the bombing of Japan during the Second World War, to mark the seventy-fifth anniversary of this event. As Fricker (2003) points out, the small concessions that have been made to include Asian performers to play the Japanese characters do not fully address the question of whether a White Western director has the right to tell tales that belong to another group. Telling the story of the horror of the bombing of Hiroshima may be an experience, like slavery or colonial exploitation, that should be reserved for those who continue to live with the legacy of these events. Howard certainly holds this view regarding *SLĀV*: 'This flippant treatment of Blackness and slavery is a consequence of universalizing projects of ostensible empathy for Black people that misapprehend Black experience – not just in its magnitude, but in its singularity' (2020: 136).

Lepage argues that these stories contain his history too, but taking the tragedies of others to create entertainment trivialises the victims of these historic events as much as it honours their memory. If theatre is the 'game of memory', then the approach taken by this director in these productions is not a winning formula in a twenty-first-century context. But perhaps the last word on this debate should go to Lepage himself, who acknowledged on Twitter that he should try harder. In January 2019, Lepage tweeted, 'As the new year begins. I resolve to do better' (2019). The theatre must be reinvented, and the pandemic crisis may have provided the perfect opportunity to create something entirely new. The success of his Stratford Festival production of *Coriolanus* on stage, in cinemas and online provides one model for the future and perhaps the opportunity to include Lepage in a new category of great twenty-first-century Shakespearean influencers. In a social media world, perhaps being a global artist will require working beyond the stage.

References

Ackerman, Marianne. (1988). 'Shakespeare? Oui!', *Saturday Night* 103 (10): 107–9.

Ackerman, Marianne. (1990). 'The Hectic Career of Robert Lepage', *Imperial Oil Review* (Winter): 14–17.

Arcand, Denis. (1980). *Jesus of Montreal*.

Aubin-Dubois, Kateri et al. (2018). 'Encore une fois, l'aventure se passera sans nous, les Autochtones?', *Le Devoir* (14 July). www.ledevoir.com/opinion/libre-opinion/532406/encore-une-fois-l-aventure-se-passera-sans-nous-les-autochtones.

Bean, Sheila. (1987). 'Central America, not Scotland, *Macbeth* Setting', *Star-Phoenix Saskatoon* (2 July): B1.

Beauchamp, Hélène. (1990). 'Appartenances et territoires: repères chronologiques', *L'Annuaire théâtral* 8 (Fall): 41–72.

Bennett, Susan. (2005). 'Shakespeare on Vacation'. In Barbara Hodgdon and W. B. Worthen, eds., *A Companion to Shakespeare and Performance*. Oxford: Wiley-Blackwell, 494–508.

Boisvert-Magnen, Olivier. (2018). 'Robert Lepage revient sur "une année de bruit et de silence"', *Voir* (28 December).

Brook, Peter. (2017). *Tip of the Tongue: Reflections on Language and Meaning*. London: Nick Hern Books.

Carson, Christie. (1993). *Moving towards 'True' Interculturalism: Experiments in Intercultural Theatre in Canada and Scotland*. Glasgow: University of Glasgow.

Carson, Christie. (2000). 'From *Dragon's Trilogy* to *The Seven Streams of the River Ota*: the Intercultural Experiments of Robert Lepage'. In Joseph I. Donohoe and Jane M. Koustas, eds., *Theater sans Frontières: Essays on the Dramatic Universe of Robert Lepage*. East Lansing: Michigan State University Press, 43–78.

Conlogue, Ray. (1990). 'A Case for the Esthetic Police', *The Globe and Mail* (June 13).

Crew, Robert. (1990). 'Wherefore Art Thou Romeo, Juliet?' *Toronto Star* (June 13).

Cunningham, Joyce, and Lefèbvre, Paul. (1980). 'Improvisation and the NHL', *Canadian Theatre Review* 25 (Winter): 79–81.

Dundjerović, Aleksandar. (2007). *The Theatricality of Robert Lepage*. Montreal: McGill-Queen's Press.

Fricker, Karen. (2003). 'The Dragons' Trilogy', *Variety* (22 June). https://variety.com/2003/legit/reviews/the-dragons-trilogy-1200540943/.

Fricker, Karen. (2020). *Robert Lepage's Original Stage Productions: Making Theatre Global*. Manchester: Manchester University Press.

Gilbert, Helen, and Joanne Tomkins. (1996). *Post-Colonial Drama: Theory, Practice, Politics*. London and New York: Routledge.

Godfrey, Stephen. (1991) 'Practice, Practice, Practice . . . Shorter Rehearsal Time Can Mean the Difference between a Dramatic Triumph and a Theatrical Fiasco', *The Globe and Mail* (October 12), p. C1.

Gunew, Sneja. (1990). 'Denaturalizing Cultural Nationalisms: Multicultural Readings of "Australia"'. In Homi K. Bhabha, ed., *Nation and Narration*. London: Routledge, 99–120.

Gunew, Sneja, and Chakravorty Spivak, Gayatri. (1989). 'Questions of Multiculturalism'. *Women's Writing in Exile*. Chapel Hill: University of North Carolina Press, 412–20.

Hamilton, Graeme. (2018) 'Montreal Jazz Festival Comes under Fire for a Show Based on Slave Songs with a Mostly White Cast', *The National Post* (3 July), https://nationalpost.com/news/canada/montreal-jazz-fest-comes-under-fire-for-a-show-based-on-slave-songs-with-a-mostly-white-cast.

Harvie, Jen. (2000). 'Transnationalism, Orientalism, and Cultural Tourism: La Trilogie des Dragons and The Seven Streams of the River Ota'. In

Joespeh I. Donohoe and Jane M. Koustas, eds., *Theater sans Frontières: Essays on the Dramatic Universe of Robert Lepage*. East Lansing: Michigan State University Press: 109–26.

Hodgdon, Barbara. (1996). 'Looking for Mr. Shakespeare after "The Revolution": Robert Lepage's Intercultural Dream Machine'. In James C. Bulman, ed., *Shakespeare, Theory and Performance*. London: Routledge, 68–91.

Hood, Sarah B. (1989/90). 'Bilingual Theatre in Canada/Le Théâtre Bilingue au Canada', *Theatrum* 16 (Winter): 9–13.

Howard, Philip S. S. (2020). 'Getting under the Skin: Antiblackness, Proximity, and Resistance in the SLĀV Affair', *Theatre Research in Canada* 41 (1): 126–48.

Hunter, Martin. (1987). 'Two-Way Traffic on the Fragile Bridge between the Theatres of Quebec and Ontario: To Be or Not to Be?' *City & Country Home* 6 (7): 18–28.

Hurley, Erin. (2011). *National Performance: Representing Quebec from Expo 67 to Céline Dion*. Toronto: University of Toronto Press.

Jacquez, Manuel Antonio. (2019). '*Coriolanus* by the Stratford Festival (Review)', *Shakespeare Bulletin* 37 (1): 111–15.

Kassam, Ashifa. (2018). 'Canadian Director behind Slave Songs Controversy Scraps New Indigenous Play', *The Guardian* (27 July), www.theguardian.com/world/2018/jul/27/canada-robert-lepage-kanata-play-indigenous-cultural-appropriation.

Knowles, Richard Paul. (1998). 'From Dream to Machine: Peter Brook, Robert Lepage and the Contemporary Shakespearean Director as (Post) modernist', *Theatre Journal* 50 (2): 189–206.

Knowles, Richard Paul. (2010). *Theatre and Interculturalism*. Basingstoke: Palgrave Macmillan.

Kulyk Keefer, Janice. (1991). 'From Dialogue to Polylogue: Canadian Transcultural Writing during the Deluge', paper presented at a conference held by the Literary Group of the British Association of Canadian Studies at the University of Leeds, 2–6 April.

Lacey, Liam. (1989). 'All the Road's a Stage for Shakespeare with a Twist: Bilingual Play Drives Home the Reality of Two Solitudes', *Globe and Mail* (7 July), A11.

Lamontagne, Gilles. (1990). 'Que donc allait faire Robert Lepage dans cette galère?' *La Presse* (14 September).

Lavender, Andy. (2001). *Hamlet in Pieces: Shakespeare Revisited by Peter Brook, Robert Lepage and Robert Wilson*. London: Bloomsbury Continuum.

Lefèbvre, Paul. (1987). 'New Filters for Creation', *Canadian Theatre Review* 52 (Fall): 30–5.

Lepage, Robert. (1993). 'Collaboration, Translation, Interpretation: Robert Lepage Interviewed by Christie Carson', *New Theatre Quarterly*, 9 (33; February): 31–6.

Lepage, Robert. (2018). Personal statement on Facebook about *SLĀV*, www.facebook.com/notes/ex-machina/position-de-robert-lepage-con cernant-slāv-robert-lepage-position-on-slāv/1891596674225125/.

Lepage, Robert. (2019). Personal Twitter post quoted in 'Quebec Playwright Robert Lepage Promises to "Do Better" after *SLĀV* Controversy', *Global News* (28 December). https://globalnews.ca/news/4799541/quebec-play wright-robert-lepage-says-controversial-slav-play-reworked/.

Lepage, Robert. (2020a). National Theatre Platform conversation with Sarah Crompton (9 March).

Lepage, Robert. (2020b). 'Director's Thoughts: *Coriolanus*, with Antoni Cimolino and Robert Lepage'. www.stratfordfestival.ca/AtHome.

Lepage, Robert, and Bonifassi, Béatrice. (2018). Joint statement on Facebook about *SLĀV*. www.facebook.com/exmachina.ca/posts/1876730789045047.

Lepage, Robert, Côté, Lorraine, Gignac, Marie, and Michaud, Marie. (1987). 'Points de repère: entretiens avec les créateurs' *Cahiers de theatre: Jeu* 45: 170–99.

References

Lieblein, Leonore. (1991). 'Political Reflections on L'Affaire Tartuffe', *Canadian Theatre Review* 67 (Summer): 66–9.

Louys, Thomas. (2018). 'Un Québécois de souche, c'est quoi?', *Le Journal du Montréal*, (13 November), www.journaldemontreal.com/2018/11/13/un-quebecois-de-souche-cest-quoi.

MacLennan, Hugh. (1945). *Two Solitudes*. Toronto, New York and Des Moines: Macmillan Canada.

McCall, Gordon. (1992). Letter to the author from Gordon McCall, dated 10 November.

McCall, Gordon. (1993). Written comments on his work sent to the author, dated 5 July.

McCall, Gordon. (1990). 'Two Solitudes: A Bilingual Romeo & Juliette', *Canadian Theatre Review* 62 (Spring): 35–41.

Molinaro, Ines. (1992). 'Multiculturalism à la Québécoise: Present condition and future challenges', paper presented at 'Quebec: The 1992 Referendum and Beyond – un Canada sans Canadiens?', conference at the University of Birmingham (16 November).

Off, Carol. (1988). 'Heritage or Cultural Evolution: Federal Policy on Multiculturalism and the Arts', *Canadian Theatre Review* 56 (Fall):5–8.

Ormsby, Robert. (2017a). 'Global Cultural Tourism at Canada's Stratford Festival: The Adventures of Pericles'. In James C. Bulman, ed., *Oxford Handbook of Shakespeare and Performance*. Oxford: Oxford University Press: 568–83.

Ormsby, Robert. (2017b). 'Shakespearean Tourism: From National Heritage to Global Culture'. *The Shakespearean World*. London: Routledge, 431–42.

Poll, Melissa. (2018). *Robert Lepage's Scenographic Dramaturgy: The Aesthetic Signature at Work*. Cham: Palgrave Macmillan.

Rempel, Byron. (1989). 'To Be or What?', *Alberta Report* (24 July).

Reynolds, James. (2019). *Robert Lepage/Ex Machina: Revolutions in Theatrical Space*. London: Methuen Drama.

'Romeo and Juliette to Tour the Country' (1990). *Globe and Mail* (14 February), C10.

'Saskatoon Director Knows How to Make Theatre Exciting' (1988). *Leader-Post Regina* (31 March).

Schechner, Richard. (1992). 'Multiculture at School', *The Drama Review* 36 (1; Spring): 7–9.

Schroeter, Ed. (1986). 'Shakespeare Show Coming to Regina', *Leader-Post Regina* (31 May), C17.

Simon, Sherry. (2000). 'Robert Lepage and the Languages of Spectacle'. In Joespeh I. Donohoe and Jane M. Koustas, eds., *Theater sans Frontières: Essays on the Dramatic Universe of Robert Lepage*. East Lansing: Michigan State University Press, 215–30.

Stockwell, Alec. (1988). 'Notes on a Crosscultural Canadian Theatre Sent from China', *Canadian Theatre Review* 56 (Fall): 40–3.

Sumney, Moses. (2018). @MosesSumney, quoted in *The National Post*. https://nationalpost.com/news/canada/montreal-jazz-fest-comes-under-fire-for-a-show-based-on-slave-songs-with-a-mostly-white-cast.

Usmiani, Renate. (1983). *Second Stage: The Alternative Theatre Movement in Canada*. Vancouver: University of British Columbia Press.

Valiante, Giuseppe. (2018). 'Robert Lepage's *SLĀV*, a Play with a Mostly White Cast Singing Slave Songs, to Run across Quebec', *Huffington Post* (11 July), www.huffingtonpost.ca/2018/07/11/slav-quebec-2019_a_23479824/.

Wallace, Robert. (1990). *Producing Marginality: Theatre Criticism in Canada*. Saskatoon, Saskatchewan: Fifth House.

Worthen, W. B. (1997). *Shakespeare and Authority of Performance*. Cambridge: Cambridge University Press.

Worthen, W. B. (2003). *Shakespeare and the Force of Modern Performance*. Cambridge: Cambridge University Press.

Cambridge Elements ⌷

Shakespeare Performance

W. B. Worthen
Barnard College

W. B. Worthen is Alice Brady Pels Professor in the Arts, and
Chair of the Theatre Department at Barnard College. He is also
co-chair of the Ph.D. Program in Theatre at Columbia
University, where he is Professor of English and Comparative
Literature.

ABOUT THE SERIES

Shakespeare Performance is a dynamic collection in a field that is both always emerging and always evanescent. Responding to the global range of Shakespeare performance today, the series launches provocative, urgent criticism for researchers, graduate students and practitioners. Publishing scholarship with a direct bearing on the contemporary contexts of Shakespeare performance, it considers specific performances, material and social practices, ideological and cultural frameworks, emerging and significant artists and performance histories.

Cambridge Elements ≡

Shakespeare Performance

Printed in the United States
By Bookmasters